GOOD NEWS GREAT JOY for ALL PEOPLE

AN ADVENT DEVOTIONAL

by Laura Cave

CONTENTS

WHY ADVENT?

I first noticed the numbness at Christmas.

New York City does Christmas like it's an Olympic sport. 50,000 lights adorn a 100-foot-tall Norway spruce in Rockefeller Center. The Rockettes high kick at Radio City while sugar plum fairies leap across the stage at Lincoln Center under showers of fake snow. Technicolor windows are unveiled with fireworks at Bergdorf's. The Salvation Army rings their bells. In Bryant Park, ice skaters loop over the lawn and the Library's great stone lions, Patience and Fortitude, sport evergreen wreaths with red bows around their necks. On the facade of Macy's, scrawled in white lights, is a single word: *Believe.*

I love this time of year, but after a few years in New York I noticed that I was bracing myself at the beginning of December. It all felt less exciting and there was a very faint sense of dread, a feeling that January would be a relief if I could just make it through. Where was this coming from?

Despite my gratitude, the monotony, the small and big griefs, and the unfulfilled longings felt heavier at Christmas. I sometimes felt lonelier. So much is unjust and unresolved in the world that the nuclear bliss of Christmas didn't feel totally honest. There was an emotional whiplash when November ran into December and the lights flipped on outside, but inside there was no corresponding spark. And the pace of life was so hectic that there was no space to process the tension I was feeling.

Each year there would be one or two quiet, almost mystical, Christmas moments that would break through to my heart. One year I went to see the *Nutcracker* at Lincoln Center. I sat with some friends near the rafters with lots of excited little girls dressed up in sparkly Mary Janes, clutching their petite purses. When the violins began the "Overture", even before the curtain lifted, tears sprang to my eyes. Another year it was during Handel's *Messiah* when the entire audience stood to their feet as the choir sang, "And He shall reign forever and ever, Hallelujah!"

The moment last year was during a concert of carols at St. Patrick's Cathedral. We got there an hour early to get decent seats but found the line already wrapped around the block. We were lucky to squeeze into standing room along the back, with our coats in one hand and small white candles in the other. People filed into every seat and lined the walls—I'd never seen so many people crammed into a church this big. At the end of the service, they dimmed the lights and we passed a small flame from neighbor to neighbor until the collective light filled even the vaulted ceilings with a warm glow as everyone sang "Silent Night." It was so beautiful it made my chest ache. The act of physically standing and singing "all is well, all is bright" with 1,000 New Yorkers, after a year of violence, terrorism, Me Too abuse allegations, and partisan squabbles, unraveled something deep in me. After weeks of the usual grind— staring at screens or down at the sidewalk, hustling up subway steps, ordering the same takeout, and reading the news— I was startled by my need for moments like this.

You could call this #adulting, growing out of our childlike naïveté. We don't believe in Santa anymore, and everyone has grown-up problems that don't magically disappear at Christmastime. The *Elf*-approach to reclaiming our childlike joy or believing in the "magic of Christmas" only seems to suggest a path backward to believing in Santa again. It offers no dignity to grown-up questions and no salve for grown-up wounds. Nostalgic fantasy is not a path forward.

If you'll permit me a childlike question, what if Christmas is capable of more than these temporary gestures toward our hearts' deepest desires? What if it contains a legitimate path to the internal alignment and social unity we glimpse in the candlelight? Deep down isn't that what we really want but are perhaps too jaded to hope for? What are we hoping for if not to come home to ourselves and to each other?

As this was happening in me, my pastor at the time invited a group of friends to read a book together called *The Ethics of Hope* by one of the most renowned experts on the theology of Christian hope, professor Jurgen Moltmann. I had just finished a masters in humanities a few years earlier, so this kind of academic reading was my jam. The book explores Christian eschatology, which is the part of theology concerned with the future, and ethical questions about the earth, our bodies, and culture in light of the gospel. After reading so many postmodern philosophers who could only explain how the Enlightenment fell apart—who could only deconstruct—I was stunned by the way the gospel put things back together.

But before I even got there, something Moltmann said on the first page of the introduction grabbed me and would not let me go. If we expect things to stay the way they are, he warns, we often ensure that they do. This makes sense. If I don't think I can get the job, I won't apply. No one can give me the job simply because my lack of hope prevented me from taking the prerequisite action for getting the job (applying). This works in subtler ways too. If I don't think anything will ever change about my neighborhood, I won't ever change anything about my neighborhood. But, he says, if we anticipate an alternative future, we'll be prepared to see and grasp our chances to make that future a reality. Hope is the prerequisite for seeing the potential in our world, and that vision is the prerequisite for action. Hope sees and seizes opportunity. We can be complicit with the status quo or we can be agents of change for the better. It all depends on how we hope.

Even while attending a church that talked about God's mission to renew the world, the alternative future God has in mind took a functional back seat to my concerns about my own future. I worried about my job, who I was dating, and carving out a foothold for myself in New York City. Most of the time it felt like being in survival mode.

But I suspect I didn't see opportunities to join God's mission because I wasn't thinking about His plans. I was thinking about my own, and I wasn't particularly happy even though most of my time was devoted to finding and protecting my own happiness. I learned to bubble wrap my hopes with weak prayers that deferred to God's will in case He decided not to say yes. I learned to expect less from people so I wouldn't be disappointed. I did this until you could hardly see the seeds of hope inside. In case you were wondering, this is how you become a cynical New Yorker. This is why I was numb to Christmas and so many other joys throughout the year. If I continued down that path, I would put myself in a position where God would have to work *without me* or even *in spite of me* to accomplish His purposes. I hated the idea that this could be true because I didn't want to miss out. I knew there was no other path to significance that could rival standing at the bleeding edge of God's Kingdom coming into the world. I had become a master of optimizing the hand I was dealt only to realize I was playing the wrong game. Whenever I get discouraged about this, I remember this verse: "Nevertheless, there will be no more gloom for those in distress… The people walking in darkness have seen a great light; on those living in the land of the shadow of death, a light has dawned." (Isa 9:1a, 2 —BSB)

Christmas is a light bulb switched on. It is *good news of great joy for all people*, just as the angels declared when they appeared to shepherds on the night of Jesus' birth. Right around the time Starbucks breaks out the red holiday cups, a much more inconspicuous tradition called Advent quietly unfolds in churches all over the world. It is an ancient liturgy designed to help us discover and rediscover the profound news of God's good plans for us and our world.

A wreath of evergreen branches is laid out with four candles nested in the branches. Much like the lights on the menorah, a new candle is lit on each of the four Sundays before Christmas. Each candle carries special significance. The candle of Hope represents the hope of the Jewish patriarchs, Abraham, Isaac, and Jacob, who were the first to put their hope in the Judeo-Christian God. The candle of Peace represents the prophets who foretold of peace between God and man through a Messiah to be born in Bethlehem. The candle of Joy evokes not only the joy of the shepherds who saw the angels' hallelujahs at Jesus' birth, but also the elation of Mary Magdalene after she encounters the risen Christ in the garden and exclaims the impossible truth, "I have seen the Lord!" The candle of Love is the last to be lit in anticipation of Christ's return when history ends with the wedding of Christ to His church and Love has its final victory over sin, Satan, death and hell, ushering in Christ's reign of love on Earth.

Since Advent is about anticipating Jesus' birth at Christmas and leaning into our hopes for His promised return, it became a pathway for me to rehabilitate my hope for my own life and for the hurting world around me. I began writing about it because I wanted to understand it and see it at work. A self-professed research nerd, my problem solving toolkit usually involves reading whatever I can get my hands on and then blabbing about it to anyone who will listen. Writing is just a more organized way of getting this information to the friends who are actually interested! It is helping me find connections to what I think about God and how I can use my hands to help make the world a better place for everyone in it. This is what I'm after for myself and for you in these pages.

Christianity holds out these four gifts—hope, peace, joy, and love—again during Advent. Unexamined, they are easy to brush off as cliché, the kinds of words you see engraved on garden signs in a gift shop. Our hearts don't come alive because of Pinterest platitudes or by cursory familiarity with multiple traditions' religious views. We have to get specific and unpack the quality and quantity of these virtues as they are offered by the gospel of Jesus Christ according to the Bible. What can we actually hope for? Is there a legitimate path to personal and social peace in the gospel? Is joy an option in spite of these challenging circumstances? Is it possible that there is a loving God who is waiting to know us? I wanted to create a safe, quiet place where anyone could dare to hear this story all the way through, to risk understanding what Christianity is really saying in a soundbite world where nuance is impossible to communicate.

We can numb ourselves with eggnog and start another year with grand ambitions to get to the gym, or we can unwrap these gifts together in light of the possibility that next year could be radically different.

Liturgy, in general, has been deemphasized in Protestant churches, and certainly a kind of going-through-the-motions liturgy has little value. But if we take on the practices and meditate on their meaning, collectively, liturgy can be a pathway from mere intellectual knowing to an emotional knowing and a communal experience where the gospel leaps off the page into hearts and communities, bringing life, love, and real change the world desperately needs. Advent may be a little old fashioned, and it may lack the sparkle of the city's more celebrated traditions, but in its rich wisdom, the liturgy of the wreath can point us to the joy we seek and help us make room in our hearts to receive it.

The path around the wreath from Hope to Love is for us to walk, to see how a baby in a manger can possibly be good news to 21st century people. Will you join us?

HOPE

Advent opens with the candle of hope, its eponymous virtue. If you've been to church services around Christmas over the years, Advent can seem like little more than an annual dusting off of seasonal content and festive songs, served with eggnog and cookies. The Sunday scripture readings bring us back to Isaiah to read the prophecies about the Christ. We turn back to the book of Luke to read the account of Jesus' birth. But with the angels that we have heard on high (again) comes a real and compelling invitation not just to the Advent season at church but to a more personal advent, the kind without a capital A, one that signifies an important arrival, the dawn of an era, a coming into being.

Advent is an opportunity to consider, for the first time perhaps, that a different future is not only possible but beginning to take shape. There is a future that does not include conflict, injustice, depression, loneliness, or death. Jesus' birth, death, and resurrection signify the beginning of the end of these old enemies of human flourishing. He will do away with them forever when He returns. Did you know that? Have you forgotten? Have you heard other people believe that and dismissed it as naïveté? Most of us could answer yes to all of those questions at one time or another. That's why Advent comes every year as an opportunity to remember and discover anew.

As Christians, we wait in the tension between what has come and what is still to come. At Christmas we receive Jesus and anticipate Jesus at the same time. If Christmas were just about looking back at the birth of a baby thousands of years ago, there would be no forward gaze. *What hope would there be?* Advent begins with hope because Jesus is not yet done with this world. He is making all things new. Better days are coming, and how we wait for them matters.

How can we be sure? The Bible is full of evidence that we can expect God to keep His word. He made covenant commitments to his people with all the force of love and permanence we commonly associate with marriage or adoption. He was faithful to those commitments even when people were unfaithful to him. He was not capricious or unpredictable like so many Greek or Roman gods. He did what He said He would do, and at His core He is Love. Lovingkindness overflows from the Trinity as the Father loves the Son loves the Spirit forever. This is how we know that God is safe to engage. His personality is stable because He has been the same yesterday, today, and tomorrow. The Scriptures are full of reminders like this one from Isaiah 46:10:

"I make known the end from the beginning,
from ancient times, what is still to come.
I say, 'My purpose will stand,
and I will do all that I please'."

So it's reasonable to suggest that God's loving and good purposes will go on with or without us—in spite of us if necessary. Whether we know Him or expect Him, He will come. But it's immensely important to Him that we both know Him and expect Him. Why?

First, because God loves you with the force of a thousand suns. He sees you fully and loves you fully. The love of God is more significant than cheap romance, more lasting than sex, more faithful than any friend, more protective than the best father, more intimate than a nursing mother. We get by on scraps of love like this. We glimpse it at the movies. He's behind the waterfall in *Last of the Mohicans* when Daniel Day-Lewis exhorts his heroine, "Stay alive! I will find you, no matter how long it takes, no matter how far, I will find you." In that long shot in *Pride and Prejudice* when Mr. Darcy stalks across the field at dawn toward Elizabeth Bennet, something springs awake in my heart and tears leap to my eyes. We were made for a God who—as we read in Song of Songs—leaps over the hills to be at our side. A God who is peering through the lattice around the garden of our lives, patiently waiting to get our attention. You may protest this is too romantic, too melodramatic, too saccharine. If you feel the protest rising, it might be worth sitting with that feeling to understand why. My point is simply: He loves you and He wants you to know it.

Second, God knows that what we expect matters. Jurgen Moltmann opens his book, *The Ethics of Hope,* with a wise reminder that when we expect that everything will stay the way it is, we often consciously or unconsciously ensure that it does. For example, if I don't think I can make a living as an artist, I'll make a living doing something else. In fact, I can never practice my craft or make a living at it because I have to work all day doing other things. We honor our doubts by calling them "realistic" or "scientific." Doubts feel safe, but they carry their own risks. Doubt can use you to create a future you don't even want.

On the contrary, when we anticipate an alternative future, Moltmann argues, we have eyes to see the possibilities in the present moment. Because we can see the potential, we're prepared to grasp our chances to make it true. When we dare to hope for better, we are prepared to pull a better future into the present. We realize God's purposes with our own hands in collaboration with Him, which we do by the power of the Holy Spirit. This is what it means to look for and *hasten* the day of the Lord's coming as Peter urges us to do (2 Pet 3:12). Isn't it wild that if we understand what God is doing—and we look to Him—He will allow us to slay some of these old dragons ourselves? If you're a Christian, look down. The Sword of the Spirit, which is the word of God, is already in your hand. The world waits wondering what will you do with it?

So we hope for Jesus' return at Advent because the God who loves us is coming into the world to renew it, and He has invited us to partner with Him in that work. God will accomplish His good plans for our future. When we hope and listen to the Spirit we become the kind of people who are prepared for this new future— the kind of people who can actually bring it about.

So this begs the question, what are you waiting for?

Maybe your sword is getting rusty and dull in your backpack. Maybe your hopes are pinned on an idol or something in your circumstances. Maybe you're just exhausted or in pain, discouraged, afraid. I'll be the first to raise my hand and identify with that, and there are so many who carry on through more loss than I've ever had to face. Brennan Manning calls the Psalmist's invitation to "Taste and see that the Lord is good" an "enormous difficulty" in the face of tragedy, betrayal, addiction, and so many other trials we experience in life. How can we hope in the face of these? Yet we must hope for something or the alternative will be despair.

Hope or Despair

On the morning of New Year's Eve a few years ago, I was on vacation in a sunny place. I sat with my coffee in a deep couch in a sunken living room that looked out on a garden full of bird chatter and a burbling fountain. I was the only one awake. It was a welcome break from the cold of New York City—and a step away from a stressful and sometimes lonely day-to-day routine. I skimmed the daily office from the Book of Common Prayer where Psalm 27 unfurled in a long scroll in the app on my phone. Near the end of the poem, verse 13 leapt off the screen at me. "I would have despaired..." it began, and the words smacked me across the forehead. Where was this in the Psalms? I'd never heard it before. But I was there. I could relate.

Somewhere along the way, I started accepting less than I hoped for because I didn't believe my hopes were possible. It had been going on for so long that I no longer knew what I really wanted. All I knew was that it wasn't working. The seed of hope was encased in scar tissue and bubble wrapped against further pain so that you couldn't even tell if it was there at all. I was nursing sour disappointment. I needed healing and a new posture toward my future. "I would have despaired" had my attention.

The verse continued, "...if I had not believed I would see the goodness of the Lord in the land of the living." Then I recognized the verse. In my Bible's normal translation the verse reads, "But I'm confident of this, I will see the goodness of the Lord in the land of the living." See the difference? As a description of the Psalmist's confidence I thought, "Well, good for you David!" I wasn't confident, so I thought the verse wasn't for me. But that morning—it was.

The Bible is translated from Hebrew to English, so there are always minor word choice differences as translators struggle to pack the precise meaning of the original language into English. But I had never seen one that so dramatically changed my understanding of a verse. I looked it up to see all the different versions from the major Bible translations. Another favorite comes from the *New King James Version*, "I had fainted, yet I believed I would see the goodness of the Lord in the land of the living." This was my verse. "I had fainted", but here was David insisting that faith was a kind of antidote to personal despair.

It's easy to believe we'll see God's goodness in heaven but believing for God's goodness here and now in this life? That took courage. I took baby steps at first. Maybe I won't ever get the things I hope for, I thought. Life is not a song that perfectly resolves every tension it holds. But what if the risk of hope could deal with the despair so that today could be better? Wasn't it the despair that was really killing me slowly inside? I decided then, that believing I would receive what I hoped for was worth the risk of not getting it, if it made all the years for the rest of my life better. I think this is part of what Elizabeth means when she prophecies over Mary during her pregnancy, "Blessed is she who believed that there would be a fulfillment of what was spoken to her from the Lord" (Luke 1:45). This became my verse for the year ahead, and it stoked my faith. It was a small hope, too small actually, in light of what God has promised us, which we'll explore in this chapter, but it was a start for me into a more hopeful frame of mind.

The verse also holds out an olive branch to the discouraged, to those who are paralyzed with despair over systemic evils like racism and misogyny, which we are so painfully confronting in our culture. Maybe you're grappling with pain or fear of economic stagnation, ecological decay, or terrorism, which are constant existential threats buzzing beneath the surface. What good news that David's hope was not for some afterlife but for the land of the living!

What would a personal advent of hope mean for you?

Israel's Hope

Hope as preparation for action and hope as an antidote to despair are wasted on false hopes that eventually die. You may believe in the magic of Christmas or that Elvis is alive, but these hopes are nonsensical and won't bring us a better future. We hope for all kinds of things over the course of our lives, and it can be tempting to read into Psalm 27:13 an implicit encouragement to hope for the good things we want (husbands, wives, children, jobs, vacations, etc.). It isn't necessarily wrong to hope for good things. The Lord delights in providing for us and giving good gifts to his children. He promises to give us the desires of our hearts when we delight in Him (Ps 37:4). But during Advent we're talking about something much bigger. A living hope is coming into the world, or as Jesus announced at the beginning of His ministry, "the kingdom of God has come near." (Mark 1:15) Jesus is the only hope that will never die. It takes knowing something about the specific claims of Christianity to understand why such a hope is both believable and good news for the imminent challenges we face both personally and as a society. And to do that we have to go back to the beginning.

The first candle of Advent is sometimes called the candle of the Patriarchs because the Jewish patriarchs were the first to hope in the Judeo-Christian God.

In the beginning we read in the book of Genesis that man and woman walked with God in a garden. This was in a time before conflict and shame entered the world. They were naked; they saw God and talked to Him as a friend. Everything was flourishing. God placed only one limitation on them, that they must not eat of a certain tree. Along came the serpent questioning Eve, she eats the fruit and gives some to Adam, and they both break God's command. Their eyes were opened and they were ashamed, clothing themselves with fig leaves and hiding from God. When He found them, He confronted them about their sin and made a provision for their shame by clothing them with animal skins. The dream of Eden ended as the once fertile earth became futile, and they could no longer live in the garden with God. As Eve stands in tears, God promised her that one day one of her descendants would crush the head of the serpent and that everything would be made right. *This was the beginning of hope.*

Many years went by and generations lived and died until God called a man named Abram. He had no children and he wasn't yet wealthy. But the Lord said to Abram, essentially, "Hey Abram, I'm gonna make you a great nation and bless you forever. You'll be a blessing to everyone. Let's go to the land I'm going to show you." Abram saw and heard God and said, "Yeah, ok. That sounds good." And he packed up and went to the land God showed him (which was Canaan).

Many more years went by until one day the Lord returned to Abram in a vision:

> "Do not be afraid, Abram. I am your shield, your very great reward." But Abram said, "Sovereign Lord, what can you give me since I remain childless … You have given me no children; so a servant in my household will be my heir." Then the word of the Lord came to him: "This man will not be your heir, but a son who is your own flesh and blood will

be your heir." He took him outside and said, "Look up at the sky and count the stars— if indeed you can count them." Then he said to him, "So shall your offspring be." (Gen 15:1-5)

Abram too lived in the tension between the call and the fulfillment of the promise. He dared to ask God how He could fulfill the promise to make him a great nation when he didn't have a single son to continue his lineage. The Lord reiterated the promise and Abram believed Him. God counted Abram's faith as righteousness. But Abram still isn't satisfied. He asks (bravely I think), "How will I know that I will possess the land?" And the Lord replies by initiating a ritual for making contracts or covenants that Abram would have recognized because it was the common way that clans and property owners made agreements in that time. He instructs Abram to gather up several animals and to cut them in half, arranging the pieces so that the blood flowed in a path between them. A king or chief of a tribe would have made the lesser party walk through the blood as a symbol of their promise, which if broken would result in his bloodshed. Abram falls into a deep sleep and sees the Lord Himself pass between the pieces twice in the form of a burning pot and a torch, in essence sealing the covenant promises and taking responsibility for the fulfillment of the contract between them.

Then God changed Abram's name, which means *exalted father,* to Abraham, which means *father of many.* Childless Abram must have felt his life was totally off-track, and here comes God upping the stakes! The promise that was yet to be fulfilled became his name. Think about how laughable that must have seemed as the years went by and Abraham the "father of many" still had no children.

In Abraham's story, we see God's desire to bless and His faithfulness to fulfill His promises, even if it's not in the timing that we expect. Yet Abraham was not immune to the kind of despair to which we can all relate. In the years between God's promise and the birth of Isaac, his wife Sarai gave her maidservant (Hagar) to her husband to conceive a child since her womb was still closed. After Hagar becomes pregnant, Sarai becomes jealous and begins to abuse her, causing her to run away into the desert.

Whenever Abraham heard from God before this, the Scriptures describe Him as the LORD (YHWH, or Yahweh). But Hagar encounters the *angel of the Lord*. The Hebrew word for angel is *mal'ak*, meaning messenger or one who is sent. Theologians believe that about a third of the 214 times this term is used in the Old Testament it refers to "christophanies," or appearances of Jesus before He was born as a human child at Bethlehem. As we learn in John 1, where the apostle John re-tells the creation narrative, Jesus was with God in the beginning. In God's command, "Let there be light," Jesus was both the light and the *logos,* or Word, which is the speaking voice in creation by which everything sprang into being and by which everything holds together. So we can recognize Jesus in these references to the *angel of the Lord* because we see His unchanging qualities, light and word, sent for God's purposes in the Old Testament.

The angel of the Lord comforts Hagar and speaks to her about her unborn son before urging her to return home. Before she goes, "She gave this name to the Lord who spoke to her: 'You are the God who sees me.'" (Gen 16:7,13) Though as a servant and a woman, she had no social standing in her own culture, we see the Lord's character as He blesses her. His actions are the same toward Hagar as they are toward Abraham and Sarah, even though Hagar's child was the fruit of Abraham and Sarah's doubt that God would fulfill His promise to them.

Indeed both Abraham and Sarah laughed at the idea that they would have a child in their old age. Yet God knew that He would make good on His promise. And their son was named Isaac, which means "he laughs." Sarah said, "God has brought me laughter, and everyone who hears about this will laugh with me." (Gen 20:6)

Later, God instructs Abraham to sacrifice his son, Isaac. Abraham is anguished but reasoned that somehow God would provide a way out. Abraham and Isaac set out with all the preparations. When Abraham took the knife to slay his son Isaac, "*the angel of the Lord* called out to him from heaven, 'Abraham! Abraham!'" (Gen 22:11). A ram caught in a nearby thicket served as the sacrifice that day. So Jesus was there, and His sacrifice was foreshadowed in the same moment.

Abraham's son Isaac married Rebekah and she gave birth to twins, Jacob and Esau. Jacob shows us another kind of hope.

When Esau was born, Jacob followed grasping his heel. That's how he got the name Jacob which means literally "he grasps the heel," or figuratively, "he deceives." As the boys grew up so did their rivalry. Isaac favored his eldest son (Esau), while Rebekah favored Jacob.

When Isaac was old and ready to pass on the blessing of inheritance to his oldest son, Rebekah conspired to help Jacob deceive Isaac and take the blessing for himself. After this, the twins became enemies and Isaac sent Jacob away. Jacob went to his mother's brother and worked for him for fourteen years to earn his wives, Leah and Rachel. In time Jacob became wealthy with livestock, servants, sons, and daughters. The Lord told him to return home. While he is on the way with his entire entourage, he hears that Esau is coming out to meet him with 400 men. Fearing conflict, Jacob splits his camp into two groups and sends the women and children safely across the Jordan.

Then he prayed boldly, reminding God of His promises:

> "O God of my father Abraham, God of my father Isaac, O Lord, who said to me, 'Go back to your country and your relatives, and I will make you prosper.' I am unworthy of all the kindness and faithfulness you have shown your servant. I had only my staff when I crossed this Jordan, but now I have become two groups. Save me, I pray, from the hand of my brother Esau, for I am afraid he will come and attack me, and also the mothers with their children. But you have said, 'I will surely make you prosper and will make your descendants like the sand of the sea, which cannot be counted.'" (Gen 32:9-12)

That evening, Jacob wrestled all night with a man he would later understand was God Himself. He experienced the same tension Abraham felt while he carried the promise of God but still had no children. Jacob's hip was wrenched painfully in the process, but he would not let go. When it was morning, Jacob said, "I will not let you go unless you bless me." (Gen 32:26) Then God blessed him and changed his name to Israel, which means "he struggles with God."

We learn from Jacob that hope is not just believing and waiting, it's active expectation. It's holding God to His promises and contending for their fulfillment. This struggle changes us.

The next day, Jacob walked toward Esau with a new name and a limp. By human standards Jacob was less capable of defending himself if this confrontation didn't go well. But his hope was stronger because he carried the blessing. After all that, we read that Esau ran to greet him and threw his arms around Jacob and kissed him. They wept happily as they were reunited in peace.

Years later Israel's family went to Egypt at the invitation of Rachel's son Joseph (of technicolor dreamcoat fame). They went to escape a famine, promising to bring Israel's bones back to Canaan one day. This led to 400 years of slavery, the same amount of time God told Abraham his people would be afflicted in Genesis 15. When Moses eventually leads the descendants of Israel's twelve sons out of Egypt toward Canaan again, they are a nation of twelve tribes. Moses went up on Mount Sinai and received the Law, a kind of new deal with the people of Israel. This covenant stipulated that if they followed the laws of God they would be blessed. If they forgot the Lord and went their own way, He would give them over to their enemies. The rest of the Old Testament follows the unfolding of this covenant, from the high of David's reign and Solomon's temple, to the low of exile in Babylon. Yet the prophets— inspired by the Holy Spirit to communicate God's messages to the people of Israel— continued to foretell of a Messiah who would bring peace and fulfill God's promise to Eve. After the last prophet died, there were 400 years of silence before Jesus was born.

A New Covenant

At the time of Jesus' birth, the Jews lived under Roman occupation. Jerusalem was the home of an elaborate temple system of sacrifices and strictly ordered worship according to Mosaic covenant law, which was by then already thousands of years old. During the years when God was silent, the people wondered when the Messiah would come and establish the kingdom of God to set them free from the brutal and corrupt leadership of the Greek and then Roman rulers. Little did they expect that God had much more in mind.

One year, one by one, Zechariah and Elizabeth, Mary and Joseph, shepherds and wise men, each had prophetic encounters with angels and heard from God in dreams. The messages signaled that events were being set in motion that would fulfill the prophecies about the Messiah with the birth of Jesus. We put ourselves in their shoes at Christmas, anticipating Jesus' birth.

We can see in the gospel accounts that Jesus was no ordinary human. He showed supernatural power by miraculous works of healing, provision, and deliverance from natural and demonic forces. He taught as a rabbi in the synagogues, explaining the Scriptures. He dared to claim that He was the son of God— a claim for which the religious leaders plotted to take His life. He perfectly fulfilled the Mosaic law because He never sinned. And just as God always does, Jesus told His disciples what would happen before it came to pass.

Jesus predicted His death three times in Luke's account alone (Luke 9:22, 44; 18:32). Death was proof that a man was not the Messiah. So with everyone's hopes set on His identity as the Messiah, these were high stakes statements Jesus was making. But He did not say simply that He would die. In John's account He elaborates that when the Son of Man is lifted up, He will draw all people to Himself (John 12:32). And although He would be handed over and killed, He explicitly stated that He would be raised from the dead on the third day. Elsewhere He says, destroy the temple and I'll rebuild it in three days. No one understood this at the time, but God was establishing His Kingdom of Life by first conquering death. This was beginning to sound like the fulfillment of God's promise to Eve.

On the night when He would be betrayed and arrested, Jesus sat down to the Passover meal with His disciples in an upper room in Jerusalem. The meal was a symbolic ritual the people of Israel had practiced for thousands of years (and still do today) in remembrance of their deliverance from slavery in Egypt, after which they were given the Mosaic covenant at Mt. Sinai. Jesus initiated a new covenant at the Passover table, which the prophet Jeremiah prophesied would come (Jer 31:31), where the bread represented His body and the cup of wine represented His blood which would be broken and poured out for them (Luke 22:20). Any student of the

Scriptures immediately sees the echoes in this moment, which harken back to God's covenant with Abraham when He passed twice through the blood of the sacrifice, when the *angel of the Lord* stayed Abraham's knife over Isaac and offered a ram instead, when the Israelites painted the blood of a lamb on their doorposts and the plague of death passed over their households in Egypt, when Moses came down from Mt. Sinai still aglow from being in the presence of the Lord and offered a new way of life to the people of God.

Jesus would go to the cross to draw us to God, to become the sacrifice, the payment that God's justice demands, so that we could have the kind of relationship that God's love demands. He walked through the blood to seal the covenant of peace. After the crowds scattered disappointed— concluding that they had just seen the death of another Messiah pretender— the grave was found empty on the third day just as Jesus said it would be.

In His death and resurrection, Jesus fulfilled God's promise to Eve by establishing victory over sin and death. He fulfilled God's promise to Abraham, that through Him all the families of Earth would be blessed (Gen 12:3). He fulfilled the law given to Moses on Mt. Sinai, and He fulfilled the terms of the New Covenant He established before His death where His broken body and poured out blood became the new pathway for the forgiveness of sins, peace with God and with one another, and ultimately resurrection life.

There is so much more to say about this, but for now we have seen that we can put our hope in God's promises because of what He has already done for us and what He will be faithful to do in the future. We can put our hope in Jesus because He became the sacrifice and took the punishment we deserved, fulfilling the terms of the new covenant with His blood. And furthermore we have hope because by the power of the Holy Spirit, Jesus was raised from the tomb to resurrection life. This same Holy Spirit was poured out on Jesus' first followers at Pentecost. The Holy Spirit indwells every believer today as a deposit of life that ensures our future resurrection and equips us to partner with God in His kingdom work.

The Holy Spirit descended on Jesus at His baptism and infused all His work with miraculous power. He healed the lepers, gave sight to the blind, made lame men walk, and fed thousands out of only a few loaves and fishes. But as Moltmann points out, those events weren't just a sign that Jesus was some kind of divine superman. They were signposts of a new creation that Jesus was breaking into the present fearful and dying world by the power of the Holy Spirit. He doesn't offer mystical, angelic, disembodied promises. He breaks supernatural life into fleshy, dusty reality to show us a taste of what's to come. He makes mud out of spit and dust and applies it to a man's eyes so he can see. People know what heaven is like because their sicknesses flee, the bleeding stops, and their stomachs are full.

When we repent and surrender our lives to Christ, we turn away from death and turn toward a living future. We are in Christ, and He is in us. We too receive the Holy Spirit and through His power, we participate in and witness the new life that is coming into the world. Moltmann clarifies that this isn't just incremental improvements to the world as it is today. It's a completely new life:

> … in Christ the kingdom has already come so close—it is actually 'at hand'—that people no longer have just to expect it, but in community with it can also already actively 'seek it', and should and can make its righteousness and beauty the goal of the way they shape the world and life. That does not mean that the kingdom of God is in their hands, but their hands are supposed to prepare the way for God's coming, and should open closed doors and lethargic hearts in expectation of his coming. (*Ethics of Hope*)

This is what it means to hope like a Christian. We enter into the New Covenant which forgives our sins and reconciles us to a loving and faithful God. It means receiving the Holy Spirit through whom we can participate in the new life of the coming kingdom of God here and now, today.

We cannot skip over the obvious question: *Have you put your hope in Jesus?*

A Hope for Today

Hope matters. It's the antidote to personal despair and it prepares us for action. We avoid the depression of disappointed hopes and the disgrace of hopes wasted on lost causes when we anticipate the faithfulness of the God who never changes and never fails to keep His word. In Jesus we have hope because we have a New Covenant, a new pathway to enter into relationship with God. When we are in Christ— having believed Him and been baptized into new life by the power of the Holy Spirit— we stand forgiven, right with God, free from shame. We receive the mind of Christ and so we become like Him, watching new life break into our disintegrating world. And we have the expectation of His promised return when sin, pain, and death will be wiped away. We'll finally dwell with God face to face.

The kingdom of God is at hand, and he is making all things new, even now. As we live like Jesus, fully human, but full of the Holy Spirit, we begin to put our hands to God's work in the world. In his book, *The Holy Longing*, Ronald Rolheiser says that, "to do anything like a Christian is to do it in view of the incarnation." So to pray is to ask God to act and then to act under the guidance and power of the Holy Spirit, to bring about the things for which we prayed. So for example, if I say, "I pray you'll be warm and well fed", but I don't offer you dinner and my couch to sleep on, I'm not praying like a Christian. His point is that we have to and we get to participate in the renewal of all things. We do this not in our own strength but at the prompting and with the energy provided by the Holy Spirit.

This hope is so central to Christian faith that Moltmann urges us not to confine it to the domain of eschatology, the part of Christianity that anticipates the future. "From first to last, Christianity is eschatology, is hope, forward looking and forward moving, and therefore also revolutionizing and transforming the present." (*Theology of Hope*).

Have you considered how a posture of hope, with the power of the Holy Spirit in you, could begin to renew the world around you?

Next we'll light the candle of Peace and examine the path to personal and social peace we find in Christ.

PEACE

In the second week of Advent we light the candle of Peace. It's a big word for such a little flame. If I'm honest, out of the four weeks of Advent, peace is the possibility that triggers the most initial skepticism in me. Just looking around, it feels hard to hope for peace. Why is peace so easy to lose and so hard to get back once it has slipped away? It has such stalwart opponents that are so tricky to untangle. How do you make peace with someone who won't listen to you? What kind of peace is possible when you or the people you love are hurting? Will anxiety ever stop visiting us in the early hours of the morning?

The beauty queen who says she wants world peace gets a laugh, but that's just cynicism laughing. Deep down we know we're just like her. We want it too, but we have no idea how. We long for peace like a river. We ache for deep internal security that allows us to operate out of our true selves without guilt, shame, or self-hatred. We crave harmony in our relationships that so often suffer threats of abandonment, rejection, or aggression. We want stabilizing peace on a geopolitical scale to turn the world into a field of opportunity for collaboration instead of conflict. We retreat to mindfulness, pushing the conflicts out of our heads while we meditate. The trouble is the timer always sounds and we have to open our eyes.

The world is not always a peaceful place, but with the eyes of hope we know one day it will be.

Christmas is the good news that peace is already here and it's how the story ends. God kept his promise to Eve that her descendant would bruise the head of evil and trample death underfoot. That moment was the "eschatological turn of the world" as Moltmann puts it. Our destiny turned from dust to glory. Christmas is so much more than "magic." It's the audacious claim that "the God of peace will soon crush Satan under your feet." (Rom 16:20)

Just like Jesus, peace has already come, yet it's still coming. It is both now and not yet. During Advent, we tell the story we're standing in from the middle.

The Problem of Peace

Whether you read it literally or poetically, Genesis tells of a time before the current time when peace was the rule and not the exception. The story traces the roots of our unrest back to what happened in the garden. There were no diseases, no bad harvests, no pests, no arguments, no hiding, and no death in the beginning. God, humankind, and nature were completely integrated and at home with one another. Nothing was out of place. Then things went terribly wrong.

In case you're not familiar with the play by play, the story goes like this. God told Adam and Eve that there was one tree from which they could not eat or they would die. The enemy in the form of a serpent slithered by and lied to them, saying that the tree would not kill them but make them wise like God. Eve wanted to be wise, and she probably had a startling new thought that God was holding out on her. She saw that the tree was good, the fruit was good, and she wanted it, so she disregarded God's command and took the fruit. She ate it, gave it to Adam, he ate it too, and the peace that permeated every part of their world was destroyed in a moment.

First, they noticed they were naked and vulnerable for the first time in their existence. Shame had arrived. So they sewed fig leaves for covering and hid from God when they heard Him walking by. The earth went from fertile to futile, producing thistles and requiring endless toil to work the land. Conflict began between man and woman. Their destiny was turned to dust. All humans to follow inherited this state of affairs and the serpent still strikes our heels in these same ways.

The root of all the disorder was disbelief. They knew God because they walked with Him face to face, and still they doubted Him. That must have stung!

Sin damages relationships, and that damage is costly to repair. The anger and offense has to go somewhere. No offense to John Lennon but we can't just imagine peace. Let's say a friend broke my trust. I can prosecute that friend and make her pay me back somehow for the wrong. I could leave the relationship broken and walk away. Or I could forgive my friend and pay the price myself every time I'm tempted to hold it against her. I'll remember that I chose to forgive and hold the pain inside instead of throwing it back at her. Every route has a toll.

If we can't imagine a toll-free peace for ourselves, then it would be illogical to expect one from a holy God who is hurt and offended by the sin in our lives. Walking away was not an option for God because He loves us. So how does God plan to make peace with us, between us, in our world? Will we pay or will He?

All our deepest longings are to get back to what they (and we) lost in Eden. Centuries before Jesus's birth, the prophets, inspired by the Holy Spirit, began to whisper of God's plan to bring us back. The God who tells us what will happen before it comes to pass has a plan and it's unfolding even now.

The Promise of Peace

A man named Isaiah was a Jewish prophet eight centuries before Jesus's birth during a time when the people of Israel were at war with the Assyrians. He experienced some of the same anxieties we experience today: the heavy burden of worry, unjust oppression, warrior's boots. But inspired by the Holy Spirit, he announces that these old patterns will end and the vestiges of war and conflict will be rolled up and burned

(Isa 9:5). This is the poetic language Isaiah uses to describe the future peace God is bringing to earth:

> The wolf will live with the lamb,
> the leopard will lie down with the goat,
> the calf and the lion and the yearling together, and
> a little child will lead them. (Isa 11:6)

Isaiah doesn't just offer a vision of peace between people, he paints a picture of a world so at peace that the very conflicts in nature are fundamentally changed. How can this be? He prophesied that a Messiah, or "Christ" in Greek, would come and not only reconcile men and women to God but restore the harmony of the garden where nature itself will be woven back together and liberated from its bondage to decay (Rom 8:21). Taken out of poetic language and put in more pragmatic terms, this means restored relationships, the end of sin and brokenness, healed bodies, a renewed earth, and life without end. What a promise! But how will God accomplish it?

We got our first glimpse of God's plan in Exodus when He allowed the blood of a sacrificed lamb to become a sign that covered His people in safety. During the last plague on the Egyptians before the people of Israel were allowed to leave captivity, the Lord told Moses that the firstborn of every family in Egypt would die. The Lord gave specific instructions for the people of Israel so that death would pass over their homes and leave their families unharmed. After sacrificing a perfect one-year-old lamb, they painted the blood on their doorposts and ate the first Passover meal. The Lord passed over their houses when the final plague took the lives of all firstborn Egyptians and Pharaoh set them free.

In the desert on their way to the promised land, God gave the people of Israel new laws. They had gone to Egypt as Israel's clan, twelve brothers and their families. But now they were a nation that had only known slavery. So these laws told them what was right and what was wrong, including the "ten commandments" which still serve as the moral foundation of a large part of the world even today. There were detailed rules for cleanliness before God and, knowing they would not be able to perfectly keep these instructions, there were detailed rules for sacrifices the people should make to restore their relationship with God after they sinned — so they could go from unclean to clean again. The blood shed on the altar was credited to them as righteousness because the animal took the place of the person who sinned. Blood atoned or made up for the sin, but the Lord didn't want His people to die; He hates death! So He allowed a substitute. This was the first pathway to peace, but it was limited and imperfect.

After King David established the city of Jerusalem and his son Solomon built the first permanent temple, the people made their sacrifices and celebrated the Passover there every year for centuries. This was still in place as the people followed Mosaic law in Isaiah's time. Yet God said through the prophet Hosea, "I desire steadfast love, not sacrifice." (Hos 6:6) The Mosaic covenant did not do away with sin and death. It didn't fulfill God's promise to Eve. The people of Israel knew they needed help. They needed a just king who could establish a lasting peace. They needed to be cleansed of sin permanently. They longed for the day of resurrection when everyone whose name was in the book of life would come alive again at the end of history— a promise they had heard proclaimed in prophecies from Daniel and Ezekiel. Throughout the Old Testament, there are whispers of One, a suffering servant, the Messiah, the Christ, who will crush the head of the serpent. Isaiah describes him:

> Surely he took up our infirmities and carried our sorrows, yet we considered him stricken by God, smitten by him, and afflicted. But he was pierced for our transgressions, he was crushed for our iniquities; the punishment that brought us peace was upon him and by his wounds we are healed. (Isa 53:4-5)

In Psalm 22, David describes this suffering in detail. There are mocking voices, pierced hands and feet, thirst, and lots cast for His garments. Another prophet, Zechariah, wrote that people would "look to the one who was pierced" and "a fountain will be open … to cleanse them from sin and impurity." (Zech 12:10; 13:1) His prophecy echoes the story of Moses who lifted a bronze snake on his staff in the desert. Anyone who was bitten by a snake could look to the snake on the staff and they were healed (Num 21:9). The prophet Jeremiah adds that the Lord will make a new covenant with the people (Jer 31:31).

This is the Messiah Isaiah announces when he declares, "a light has dawned on those who were living in a deep darkness." (Isa 9:2) When they could not see their way out, suddenly a light shines on them. All of this points to a plan for peace that is God's initiative, a plan where He would carry the cost of reconciliation. Just as the Lord passed between the pieces when He made His covenant with Abraham, the Lord seemed to be taking on the expense, the shed blood, that would be required to make the relationship between God, man, woman, and nature right again.

* * *

All of this blood and sacrifice sounds so foreign to our modern ears, but we too go to elaborate and costly lengths to deal with our shame and make ourselves acceptable in our own eyes and in the eyes of others. We may not try to pay for our shame and purchase new peace with the blood of animals, but we certainly try to manage sin and its repercussions in other ways. We seek to placate those we have offended, we hide the parts of ourselves which are unacceptable or unclean, we pay for our wrongdoings in the form of parking tickets and court settlements. But still all of these attempts often fall short of truly satisfying those we have hurt or cleansing us from what we have done. There is no one who can truly absorb the full weight of these wounds in our place, so that we can then make true, lasting peace with each other,

And just like the ancient Israelites, we too live under impossible expectations and unattainable perfectionism that can be a heavy burden on our backs. It's easy to look at the Mosaic law and think we're so evolved. Why does God have such high standards? Why did they spend their lives making sacrifices to make up for falling short? As soon as I've typed the question, I see things haven't changed all that much. This is actually the heart of all religion: striving to be good enough to cover up our guilt and shame, to justify our existence. And even secular culture plays the game.

You know how it goes. Try to excel at work, eat clean, get to the gym, read all the things, support your family, raise your children right, be a good friend— the list of requirements to be a good person never end. If you're a Christian it's easy to stay in this mode and simply pile on gratitude and Bible study and more. We can and should do many of these things freely with joy. These practices aren't bad, but so often they become tools to cover up shame. We wear them like masks so people can't really see us and we wonder why we so often end up estranged from each other, lonely, and numb, even at Christmas! We can play this performance game or we can opt out in rebellion, but these responses don't actually help us take our masks off. None of our masks can give us the deep peace we long for. Only God can do such a miraculous work. Only He can be the true peacemaker and the fulfillment of the Old Testament promises.

The Prince of Peace

After the last prophets of the Old Testament died, there were no more messages from God for 400 years. God was silent. He called no more men or women to be prophets and He sent no messages to the people by way of the Holy Spirit. Until one year, a priest named Zechariah was serving in the Temple and when he went in to offer the sacrifice as usual, he saw an angel of the Lord. The angel told him that he would have a son who would be full of the Holy Spirit and who would prepare the people of Israel, in the spirit and power of Elijah, for the Lord's arrival (Luke 1:17). This was a direct reference to Malachi 4:5, which promised that Elijah would precede the day of the Lord.

The years of silence were over.

A few months later, Luke tells us that the angel Gabriel appeared to Mary to tell her that she had found favor with God and would give birth to a son who would be the Christ. The Holy Spirit would overshadow her, and the child would be called holy, the Son of God. Notice the details Gabriel gives Mary about this miraculous child:

> Do not be afraid, Mary, for you have found favor with God. And behold, you will conceive in your womb and bear a son, and you shall call his name Jesus. He will be great and will be called the Son of the Most High. And the Lord God will give him the throne of his father David, and he will reign over the house of Jacob forever, and of his kingdom there will be no end. (Luke 1:30-33)

Notice how Gabriel's words echo Isaiah 9:6-7:

> For to us a child is born,
> to us a son is given;
> and the government will be upon his shoulder,
> and his name will be called
> Wonderful Counselor, Mighty God
> Everlasting Father, Prince of Peace.
> Of the increase of his government and of peace
> there will be no end,
> on the throne of David and over his kingdom,
> to establish it and uphold it
> with justice and with righteousness
> from this time forth and forevermore.

The zeal of the Lord of hosts will do this.

A child. And the government will be on this child's shoulders. This child will be called Prince of Peace. Isn't it interesting that Isaiah didn't say "a warrior will come"? God didn't send Jesus as a man, fully formed like Athena sprung from the head of Zeus. Instead, a child is given. God enters the world as a helpless baby.

Have you ever held a baby? There's a kind of focus and openness that comes with holding a newborn. We look intently into their faces and they search ours. They are so innocent, so completely non-threatening. It feels wonderful to be seen by them. A few months later, they smile at you and it's like the sun coming out from behind a cloud. Isn't it curious that God enters the human race this way? The Christ who came to liberate us from sin and establish peace, was born in a stable in Bethlehem with absolutely no defenses of any kind. This seems totally paradoxical but Jurgen Moltmann explains:

> This future [liberation] is wholly and entirely God's initiative. That is why it is so totally different from our human plans and possibilities ... On the human side all we see here is weakness and helplessness. It is not the pride and strength of the grown man which are proclaimed the threshold of the kingdom, but the defenselessness and the hope of the child.

The kingdom of peace comes through a child and liberation is bestowed on the people who become as children: disarming others through their defenselessness. Jesus comes to us at

peace & defense don't co-exist

Christmas as a newborn, dissolving our defenses. Maybe babies scare you because you quite like your defenses— you've become quite attached to them. Babies are innocent of such sophistication, and their fragility demands protection. As a child born of a virgin, Jesus didn't inherit the curse of Adam's sin, so He alone could lead the way into a new kind of human life. And He is inviting us in: "Truly, I say to you, unless you turn and become like children, you will never enter the kingdom of heaven." (Matt 18:3) This is why Jesus told Nicodemus that unless he is born again he cannot see the kingdom of God (John 3:3).

him

But Jesus does not stay a baby forever. In obedience to the Father, Jesus goes on to initiate God's new covenant with humanity by reinterpreting the Passover feast around himself— His body is the bread broken for us, and His blood is the cup of the new covenant shed for us. Jesus is then arrested, beaten, mocked, and crucified, and the soldiers cast lots for His garments just as the prophets foretold. Just before His death, He cried out in a loud voice the opening refrain of Psalm 22, in which David had prophetically understood the suffering of the Messiah a thousand years before that moment: "My God, my God, why have you forsaken me?" In His death, Jesus became the unblemished lamb of the passover feast. His blood is the substitute payment that can change us from unclean to clean. It is the sign that death will pass over us.

Jesus's death is so unlike the deaths most men die. Though Jesus was the victim of an unjust trial and brutal killing, He does not use His victimhood as power over others. As Richard Rohr explains:

> Jesus receives our hatred and does not return it. He suffers and does not make the other suffer. He does not first look at changing others, but pays the price of change within himself. He absorbs the mystery of human sin rather than passing it on. He does not use his suffering and death as power over others to punish them but as power for others to transform them.

When Abraham believed, God credited his faith as righteousness (Gen 15:6). Likewise when we put down our elaborate efforts to restore our inner peace and instead put our faith in Jesus, we are justified before God and changed. Our sin is forgotten, as it was paid for by Christ on the cross. Like those who looked to the bronze snake that was lifted up in the wilderness, when we look to Jesus we are healed of our waywardness:

> Therefore, if anyone is in Christ, that person is a new creation. The old is gone; the new is here! All this is from God who reconciled us to himself through Christ, not counting people's sins against them. And he has committed to us the ministry of reconciliation. We are therefore Christ's ambassadors, as though God were making his appeal through us. We implore you on Christ's behalf: Be reconciled to God. (2 Cor 5:17-21)

This isn't an invitation into foolishness or immaturity. It's an invitation into a new kind of wisdom that is naive to sin and cynicism, and into a new humanity that is capable of a future. In his first letter to the Corinthians, the apostle Paul calls Jesus the last Adam because He is the first born of a new humanity, people whose destiny is tied up with Jesus's future (1 Cor 15:45).

God's plan for reconciliation did not stop with Jesus's death, for what peace is there when that old thief still separates us from those we love? When Jesus had sacrificed everything in obedience to the Father, His body was broken and He descended into Hell under the weight of the sin of all humanity. But by the power of the Holy Spirit, He was raised from the dead. He became a signpost of our future, breaking into the present moment.

On that exceptional morning, to whom did He appear first? It wasn't the authorities who'd ordered Him crucified or the pharisees who plotted His death. It wasn't even the disciples whom He loved. First, it was to a formerly-possessed woman in tears, in the garden beside His tomb. It must have been with such restrained joy that Jesus said to Mary Magdalene, "Woman, why are you weeping?" At first she thought He was the gardener. Jesus, as both God and the last Adam, stood before Mary—a woman just like that first Eve—and He proclaimed the good news. God, man, and woman were reconciled in the garden that day, which marked the eschatological turn of the world from a future marked by death to a future capable of life.

The Pathway to Peace

Jesus doesn't just make a path for reconciliation with God, He also offers a pathway to peace for all people with each other.

While the people of Israel were under the Mosaic covenant, anyone outside the people of Israel didn't have access to the path of reconciliation because they couldn't go into the Temple. But the new covenant in Jesus's blood had no such requirement, so He offers a path to unity over and against all the old sources of division. Paul explains further in his letter to the Ephesians:

> But now in Christ Jesus you who once were far off have been brought near by the blood of Christ. For he himself is our peace, who has made us both one and has broken down in his flesh the dividing wall of hostility by abolishing the law of commandments expressed in ordinance, that he might create in himself one new man in place of the two, so making peace, and might reconcile us both to God in one body through the cross … In him you also are being built together into a dwelling place for God by the Spirit. (Eph 2:13-16a, 22)

Through the death and resurrection of Jesus, God fulfilled all His covenant promises and made a new pathway of peace for all people. In Christ there is "neither Jew nor Greek, there is neither slave nor free, there is no male and female" for all have direct access to the Father, all have the indwelling Holy Spirit (Gal 3:28). All are made one in the new humanity of those who are in Christ. We are still grappling with racism and misogyny, but unity is possible because of Jesus. This process is not finished, not even in the church among those who are reconciled to Christ, but by faith we know the day is coming, and as we participate in obedience to the Father and through the power of the Holy Spirit with the changes He is working in us, wholeness and reconciliation are possible.

The Church has an important role to play here. As people who have believed in Jesus, together we become the metaphorical body of Christ, the family and household of God, a colony of heaven on earth where God is present by his Holy Spirit and the future breaks into the present in the form of healing and restoration.

The Peacemaking Church

Jesus promised His disciples, "Peace I leave with you; my peace I give to you. Not as the world gives do I give to you. Let not your hearts be troubled, neither let them be afraid." (John 14:27)

Christ reconciled us to God through His death on the cross, and He has made us peacemakers of the most unexpected sort: forgiving and childlike. In Christ we receive a whole new life, becoming children of God and citizens of heaven (Rom 8:16; Phil 3:20). Jesus went away promising that He was preparing a place for us. He promised to return, bringing with Him the final victory and a new, peaceful earth. As Christians, we are not just individuals who share the same ideas. We are a new people living out a true story under a different authority than the world around us. If this sounds political, that's because it is.

> And they admitted that they were aliens and
> strangers on earth. People who say such things

show that they are looking for a country of their own. If they had been thinking of the country they had left, they would have had opportunity to return. Instead, they were longing for a better country—a heavenly one. Therefore God is not ashamed to be called their God, for He has prepared a city for them. (Heb 11:13a-16)

At Christmas, we long for Jesus's return and all the renewal that will come with Him. We long for the goodness and glory of God to reign in New York City as it is in heaven. While we wait and hasten this coming reality, the question arises: How do we work for the peace of the city?

Two Duke University theologians, Stanley Hauerwas and William Willemon discuss the pitfalls and possibilities for how the church can do this. One approach, they explain, is to focus on renewing society through social justice. Indeed, we are commanded to care for the poor and sick, to welcome the foreigner, to visit those in prison. But when we take up the mantle of peacemaking without proclaiming Christ, we can give the impression that peace is possible without Him. Another approach is to focus only on individual conversion because when people encounter the gospel, they will be at peace with God. Of course we must proclaim the gospel! But if we only focus on evangelism, we won't have any alternative social ethic to offer our hurting world.

They conclude and argue that the best way the Church can offer peace to the world is to be the Church: a visible, alternative society that puts the peace of God on display before the nations and invites them in. This is how we are to "come out from them and be separate" while also being "a light to the nations" (2 Cor 6:17; Isa 49:6). Rather than trying to grab the power of the world, they urge the Church to reconnect with its own power, the Holy Spirit, and to be the place where people live in unity, forgiving each other just as Christ has forgiven us. This is why it is so vital that we stand guard against racism, misogyny, and other sins inside the Church. But we also recognize that we are a people in process— just like the disciples. One minute Peter is walking on water toward Jesus and the next he is sinking in fear and doubt. God's grace covers us, and his Spirit empowers us toward these ends. By faith we know that this hoped for reality will come, and we participate with the Lord in it whenever we see opportunity.

Peace on Earth

By His death and resurrection Jesus reconciles us to God and to each other, but we also see nature respond to Him in miraculous ways. This gives us an idea of what it will be like when more of the anticipated future God has promised breaks into the present, and when the promises of Isaiah 11:6 finally come to pass.

At His baptism, Jesus receives the Holy Spirit and begins His public ministry. From that day on, He performs miracles and signs that defy the laws of nature. What is this about? Read the gospels and it seems like everywhere He went water became wine, the lame walked, the blind could see, bread and fish multiply to feed the hungry, demons leave people, and bleeding stops just by touching the hem of Jesus's robe. I used to think that Jesus's miracles were proof of His divinity, that He was really God and man. They do prove His dual-nature, but I think there's something more to them. The miracles of Jesus point to another reality— the reality of the kingdom, which is like the garden, marked by health and *shalom* (wholeness, peace), and which is held together by His speaking voice. In that world, such miracles are not exceptional. They will be normal reality.

This is why the prophet Isaiah says that when the Messiah comes: "The wolf will live with the lamb, the leopard will lie down with the goat, the calf and the lion and the yearling together; and a little child will lead them. ... They will neither harm nor destroy on all my holy mountain, for the earth will be filled with the knowledge of the LORD as the waters cover the sea." (Isa 11:6, 9)

As Pastor Suzy Silk explains, when the Prince of Peace comes to the earth, He brings the peace of God's kingdom with Him. The sick are healed, because His health drives out their sickness. The blind can see, because He opens their eyes with the mud He has spit in. The fish respond to His command because He is the new Adam who brings peace to the created world. And the waters calm and rise to hold His stepping feet, because at the sound of Jesus's voice they hear the peaceful voice of their creator. In Jesus— the second Adam and the promised seed of Eve— the curse that has plagued the ground since the Fall is finally lifted (Rom 8:19-21). Jesus brings peace on earth among mankind and also peace to the earth itself.

We see the promise of peace on earth and the questions it provokes quite clearly in one of Jesus's miracles. Jesus and His disciples are out in a boat on the Sea of Galilee. Jesus is asleep on a cushion, after a long day of proclaiming the kingdom and healing the sick. When the boat reaches the middle of the lake, a storm appears with a strong windstorm sending huge waves crashing into the boat. As the winds and waves pick up their ferocity, the disciples (some of whom were seasoned fishermen) begin to panic. But Jesus is still asleep, totally unfazed by what nature is doing.

The disciples, afraid of drowning, wake Jesus up. Certain they are about to die, they ask Him (I imagine furiously), "Don't you care that we are perishing?" Jesus then wakes up and speaks to the wind and the sea these simple words, "Peace! Be still!" Suddenly everything is calm.

In the aftermath of the storm and the sudden peace all around them, the disciples ask the question which I think we all must wrestle with: "Who then is this, that even the wind and the waves obey him?" (Mark 4:41)

Our world is often filled with natural, political, and personal storms. Often times, even at Christmas, we may feel like the winds and waves of brokenness, shame, and corruption are about to overtake us. In the midst of this, where will we turn to find peace and security?

Christmas is an invitation to discover Jesus Christ: the Prince of Peace. His life is a gift to you as disarming as a child, an acceptable sacrifice for your sin, and a path to legitimate peace inside and outside with God and with man. If you can hear this, and if something is stirring inside you saying yes, then "Behold, now is the time of favor; now is the day of salvation." (2 Cor 6:2, BSB) Put your faith in Jesus and receive His peace.

JOY

After you left
I jumped up and down,
I stared into space.
In those days I was starving for happiness.
So, say it was both silly and serious.
Say it was the first warm sting of possibility.
Say I sensed the spreading warmth of joy.

—from *The First Day* by Mary Oliver

Originally, Advent was intended as a somber period of reflection and fasting in preparation for Christmas joy. It was a fast before the feast, similar to Lent, which precedes Easter. In the cold, dark days of December, the faithful longed for Christ's return, but halfway through the season there is a turning point. The third Sunday of Advent has a special name: Gaudete Sunday, which is named after the latin word for 'rejoice'. The traditional liturgy for mass begins with Paul's exhortation to the Philippians:

> Rejoice in the Lord always. I will say it again: Rejoice! (Phil 4:4)

It's for this reason that the third candle on the Advent wreath is pink, rather than blue or lavender. Both are liturgical colors from the vestments worn by priests, but I like seeing them in this order because it seems to follow the sunrise. The light dawned with hope and grew brighter with the promise of peace, but now the sun has climbed over the horizon and it lights up the sky with color. The brightening sky of the early dawn provides visibility after a long, dark night, but it isn't until the sun's rays land on your skin that you can feel the warmth. Dawn is actually cold until that happens.

Your Advent journey might feel like this, in some ways. If you've followed along this far, you've slogged through a lot of theology and a lot of the biblical narrative, but these aren't much more than words until they come alive for you personally. If they're still just ideas, they might be piled in your lap in a heap. Maybe you're not sure what to make of them. The world may still seem grey. You may feel detached, like nothing is stirring inside you. This is perhaps a roundabout way of saying, this book alone won't change your life. Only an encounter with Jesus can do that.

My first instinct when I want to understand something is to read up on it, to get smarter about a subject. I want to gather all the facts, wrap my head around it, and build a map inside my mind. But there are a lot of things in life we can't really understand this way. You can read every book about tennis, but without hours of instruction and practice you'll be a lousy player. You can study books about parenting, but you'll never really know about it until you've held your newborn in your arms and lived the day to day process of raising a child.

I know first hand that information alone won't change you. It didn't change me. I grew up going to church. By now, that means I've gone to church for almost two thousand Sundays. My faith didn't really became my own until I was thirteen. Nothing dramatic happened, but the pieces clicked into place and from then on I knew that I knew that I knew God was real, that He loved me, and that Jesus had died for me. I understood that He had been quietly pursuing me for my whole life, and I was hungry to understand and experience God. I wanted to be as close to Him as possible. I was taught well by pastors all over the U.S. from Christian Missionary Alliance, Presbyterian, Episcopal, and non-denominational churches. I went on missions trips and witnessed the miraculous. But by the time I was in my twenties, I was a stressed out grad student at NYU and a young woman trying to carve out a career and a place to belong in New York City. I knew a lot about God, but to be honest I lacked confidence in His character. I hadn't had enough personal encounters with God to help me withstand the pressures around me and I didn't have a very big toolbox. I knew a lot about hermeneutics and apologetics but next to nothing about prayer, contemplation, and worship. I knew what God said about me—that I was beloved, forgiven, accepted—but what other people thought about me was more visceral. And I lived reacting to those things, rather than being rooted in who God was and who He said I was.

Of course ideas have limited effect. You are more than a brain on a stick. You're someone with emotions, habits, and relationships. And, importantly, God is not an idea for you to consider or debate. He is a triune person: Father, Son, and Spirit. He is not an ego in the sky. He is three in one, a perfectly coordinated dance of unbroken joy. Does it surprise you to hear that God is the happiest being in the universe? Look at what happens when heaven's joy spills over onto the earth, onto bewildered men and women just like us.

The Happiness of Heaven

In Luke 2 we read that Jesus was born in Bethlehem during a census, which had been ordered by Caesar Augustus. It was the worst possible timing for Mary, whose pregnancy was full term. She and Joseph had to travel from Nazareth in Galilee to be counted in Bethlehem, just south of Jerusalem, because their families were from the line of David. The distance was around 80 miles, about the same distance from Philadelphia to New York City. They famously found no room to stay at the inns, so had to settle in a humble stable. When he was born, the baby Jesus was swaddled and placed in an animal feeding trough. It may have seemed like an ordinary birth during a hectic time to some, but the inhabitants of heaven could not contain themselves.

In the Judean hills nearby, angels appeared to shepherds to bring "good news of great joy for all people." (Luke 2:10)

It's hard to imagine such an angelic display. Certainly these poor shepherds had zero expectation that such an event was plausible or probable. Just imagine watching over a herd of sheep in the countryside at night. Perhaps you're near a small campfire for warmth. You keep your back to the flames, and your eyes adjust to the cool darkness scouting for wolves, their eyes glinting in the firelight. Then suddenly an angel appears and you see the glory of the Lord shining all around you! That blinding, startling appearance must have been absolutely terrifying.

> Fear not, for behold I bring you good news of great joy that will be for all the people. For unto you is born this day in the City of David a Savior who is Christ the Lord. (Luke 2:10)

For anyone familiar with the prophecy about the coming Messiah in Isaiah 9, as these shepherds a few short miles outside of Jerusalem must have been, this was indeed amazing news. Today was the day! The promised child had been born! The One they had been waiting for had arrived.

Next, the Scriptures recount that a great multitude of heavenly hosts appeared. They were praising God with shouts of, "Glory to God in the highest, and on earth peace among those with whom He is pleased!" (Luke 2:14) It must have been as brilliant as the Fourth of July over the East River. The air must have been ringing with sound, as the words echoed through the valleys and ricocheted off the hills. Heaven quite literally lost itself in joyful celebration in that moment. The scene echoes the Lord's description of the moment of creation when He questions Job, "Where were you when I laid the foundations of the earth...when the morning stars sang together and all the sons of God shouted for joy?" (Job 38:7) It seems that heaven's joyful roar could not help but spill over onto the inhabitants of the earth on the night of Jesus's birth.

Encountering Joy

The gospel of Luke tells us that when Elizabeth heard Mary's greeting, the baby in her womb leaped for joy (Luke 1:41). This baby was John the Baptist who knew, even in utero, that he was in the proximity of the Emmanuel, God with us. As a man, John the Baptist spent his life preparing the way for Jesus by calling people to repentance and baptizing them in the River Jordan. He would eventually baptize Jesus too, with a similar moment of recognition when he saw the Holy Spirit descend and rest on Jesus like a dove (John 1:32).

Likewise, the shepherds couldn't just go back to their shift work on the night of Jesus' birth. They couldn't shrug their shoulders, question the emotional exuberance of the angels and go back to work on Monday as if nothing had happened. They had to respond. So they searched the city until they found the baby Jesus just as the angels had described Him.

Magi from the east followed a star that led them to Bethlehem, and were overjoyed to have found the baby King (Matt 2:10). They brought Jesus expensive gifts, the kind of extravagance you never mind when it's for someone you love. Mary and Joseph must have been so encouraged by these strange visitors, who confirmed what they also had been told by the angel Gabriel: that this child was the Christ who had been promised.

When Joseph and Mary presented Jesus at the temple in Jerusalem, they encountered Simeon, who had been waiting patiently for the Messiah all his life. By the power of the Holy Spirit, Simeon recognized that this child Jesus was the promised Christ and he praised God with a joyful prophetic declaration. Likewise, a widow prophetess named Anna, who worshipped God in the temple day and night, gave thanks to God and told everyone who was waiting for the Messiah about Jesus (Luke 2:25-38).

It's not enough just to hope for God's promises or to anticipate His peace. It's not even enough to know about Jesus. We need a heart-leaping encounter where in our own personal language, God meets us and says hello. This can be spectacular or subtle. A friend of mine describes the day she met God as "Holy Spirit fireworks", but that's not everyone's experience. It wasn't mine.

I once read that God is more domestic than monastic, that He is not hidden away in a church, but He's there in the feeling you get around a dinner table of loved ones or when the doorbell rings because your friend has just arrived. The most joyful encounters always feel a bit like reunions, don't they? Have you ever met someone and instantly felt like you've known them your whole life? The Bible is full of joyful encounters and homecomings. There is so much energy in those moments. We honor them with dinner reservations, we stay out too late, we set an extra place at the table for dinner.

We are still buzzing when the last guest leaves and all the candles are still burning.

I sometimes see little vignettes when I pray, like short little scenes from a movie. Some of them repeat or build on previous visions like recurring daydreams. I'm a visual learner, so I think it's my brain's way of imagining things my spirit knows but that I can't see with my eyes. Often I'll be in the middle of my day, maybe walking down the street or in a room full of people, and I'll sense the Lord catch my attention. In my mind's eye, I'm in a ballroom, dancing with some gentleman I never see because I'm looking over his shoulder. We twirl around among many other couples in a kind of waltz, which is ironic because I have no idea how to waltz. Then in the middle of the song, I see the Lord over my dance partner's shoulder. I couldn't tell you what He looks like but my spirit knows Him and my stomach flips happily. I'm suddenly totally uninterested in my dance partner or whatever else is going on in the room. Other concerns and appetites fade away. I turn my head to keep my eyes on the Lord in the crowd, as my partner and I swirl around the dance floor. Eventually, He always asks to cut in.

Don't we long for moments like this? Moments that inspire a kind of happy dance that's impossible to contain? God always seems to evoke this kind of reaction from the people who know Him well.

Remember King David, the shepherd-poet warrior-king? David was anointed by the prophet Samuel to become king of Israel when he was a boy. At that moment the Spirit of the Lord "came upon him with power." (1 Sam 16:13) But David's road to the throne was not easy. When he had finally united the nation, conquered Jerusalem and the Philistines, and established peace after years of conflict, he brought the Ark of the Lord into his new capital city, and was dancing with all his might at the head of the procession because of all that God had done. But David's wife Michal, the daughter of the previous king, looked down from her window with disdain for him. "How the king of Israel has distinguished himself today, disrobing in the sight of the slave girls of his servants as any vulgar fellow would!" (2 Sam 6:20) Can you hear the sarcasm in her voice?

But David responds, "I will celebrate before the Lord. I will become even more undignified than this." (2 Sam 6:22) My fear of looking undignified has held me back in worship and in moments when the Spirit has prompted me to approach someone and speak to them. In Psalm 16 David praises God and shows us where his joy comes from:

> You make known to me the path of life, in your presence is fullness of joy, at your right hand are pleasures forevermore. (Ps 16:11)

David knew that joy came from encountering the Lord, and he spent so much time in the Lord's presence that his joy was filled to overflowing. Have you had your fill? Are you satisfied? Joy is available to you in the Lord's presence, and it will fill you until you overflow onto the people around you. It may be undignified, but the good news is by the time it happens to you, like David, you won't care.

Reunion Rejoicing

If anything can top the joy of encounter, it must be the joy of reconciliation, the elation of a reunion after a relationship was lost.

In Jesus's famous parable, the Prodigal Son, the father catches a glimpse of his son returning home and runs out to meet him on the road, his sandals pounding the dust. In Song of Songs the lover leaps across the mountains, bounding over the hills toward his beloved. Mary and Joseph search all Jerusalem for three days until they find a young Jesus sitting in the Temple among the teachers. Jesus finds Mary Magdalene in the garden on Easter morning.

The late Irish poet, theologian, and philosopher John O'Donohue tells Krista Tippett during her *One Being* podcast (in a wonderful Irish brogue) that all spirituality is a kind of homecoming. While the mind is always separating *what is* from *what is not*, the imagination insists on a kind of 'justice of wholeness'. The imagination is always sistering the dualities of life, things long separated, bringing them together in "creative and critical harmony," O'Donohue says. In this sense, we are very much committed to telling stories with happy endings. And there is nothing better than a true story.

In Jesus, we see this same reconciliation. After Adam and Eve left the Garden of Eden, God and humans, heaven and earth had previously only touched each other in the Holy of Holies, in the Temple, on Yom Kippur, when the high priest would sprinkle the blood of a sacrificed bull in the presence of God to make atonement for the people. But when Jesus, who was both God and man, became the atoning sacrifice on the cross, He made the entire system of temple sacrifice obsolete. He raised up a new temple, His body, in three days when He rose from the dead, just as He said He would (John 2:19; Mark 14:58; Matt 26:61). From the moment of Jesus's death, the curtain surrounding the Holy of Holies was torn in two, and the temple was relocated to the hearts of believing humans, who have received the indwelling of the Holy Spirit.

Not only is harmony between our souls and His Spirit possible now, but there is a greater reunion in store for those who are in Christ. For now "we see but a poor reflection as in a mirror; then we shall see face to face. Now I know in part; then I shall know fully, even as I am fully known." (1 Cor 13:12)

Rejoice, Rejoice

The subject of joy is challenging when you're in the midst of difficult circumstances. I remember a season when I was working full time and hustling to deliver my master's thesis and finish my graduate degree. The stress was real and it went on for a long time. When I finally turned in my paper and got my diploma, it took awhile for me to get out of the emotional rut of stress that I'd been in. God understands this and does some of the work for us. In the Psalms, David testifies, "You turned my wailing into dancing. You removed my sackcloth and clothed me with joy." (Ps 30:11) No matter your circumstances, the Lord would like to clothe you with joy. Will you let Him?

In Philippians, the so-called "Epistle of Joy," Paul uses the words joy and rejoice 14 times, and closes with the double exhortation in chapter four: "Rejoice in the Lord always. I will say it again: Rejoice!" (Phil 4:4) Ever wonder why he tells them twice? Maybe the Philippians needed to hear it twice, or maybe Paul needed to write it! Maybe the joy wasn't coming naturally. We can see the reasons why in the book of Acts. Things were not going well for the Philippians or for Paul.

In Acts 16 we read that Paul went to Philippi after he had a vision in a dream. A man from Macedonia pleaded for him to come and help them, so in obedience Paul took his companions and went. When they arrived, they met Lydia, who became a believer along with her entire household. In the days that followed, there was a slave girl who was possessed by a spirit of divination. She kept on following them and shouting that Paul and his companions were servants of God proclaiming salvation. While this was true, perhaps it was not the way Paul wanted to open his conversations, so he became increasingly annoyed and cast the demon out of her. Her masters, who'd previously made great sums of money off her fortune-telling powers, were incensed and hauled Paul into court. The magistrates had him and Silas beaten and thrown into prison.

Around midnight, we're told, Paul and Silas were praying and singing songs to God in their prison cell. Suddenly there was an earthquake. The prison doors were opened and everyone's shackles were unfastened. The jailer was so startled that he and his entire household became believers that night. The church of Philippi grew rapidly through the radical work of the Holy Spirit from that day forward. Isn't it profound that praise from a prison cell had the power to unleash the power of the Holy Spirit, not only in the physical to unlock doors and loose chains, but also in the spiritual to bring whole families into a saving encounter with Jesus?

Then many years later, Paul writes the book of Philippians to Lydia, the jailer, and the rest of the Philippian church from Rome, where he is in chains again under house arrest. Since he left them, he had been flogged, imprisoned, and shipwrecked. The Philippian church was concerned, to put it mildly, so they sent a brother, Epaphroditus, with gifts and provisions for Paul. Epaphroditus arrived but got sick after the long journey and nearly died.

In spite of all this, again Paul rejoices! He prays with joy because he is confident that God will complete the work He started in them (Phil 1:6). He rejoices in the Lord despite his chains because he knows that what has happened to him will work out for his deliverance (Phil 1:19). He also rejoices at the prospect of their future joy in Christ, when they can be together again (Phil 1:26). So in his letter Paul is modeling for his friends the rejoicing he urges them to do. It has nothing to do with his present circumstances and everything to do with who he knows God to be. His faith in God's character and his encounters with the presence of the Lord in worship give him a completely different perspective on his situation than we would expect.

Paul shows us that joy is not only possible but effective even when our efforts appear frustrated or cut short, even when we're crushed by disappointment, even when we're abandoned or wounded through no fault of our own. Even in the prisons of loneliness, addiction, or loss, praise can open doors because God is committed to this truth: whatever was intended for evil, God will use for your good (Gen 50:20, Rom 8:28). Joy is not just a fruit of circumstance but a fruit of the Spirit, which comforts us in our distress. This is how James can dare to exhort us:

> Count it all joy, my brothers, when you meet trials of various kinds, for you know that the testing of your faith produces steadfastness. And let steadfastness have its full effect, that you may be perfect and complete, lacking in nothing. (Jas 1:2-4)

Good News About Great Joy

From time to time, if we're lucky, we experience profound joys in this life. Can you recall any moments like that? Maybe it was your first car, walking across the stage at graduation, your wedding day, the births of your children, or the first time you visited Paris. We catch glimpses of joy but they always fade with familiarity. The car gets a scratch and starts to break down; you have a degree but now you need a job; the family becomes the new normal.

We know somehow, as C.S. Lewis puts it in *Mere Christianity*, that "the longings which arise in us when we first fall in love or first think of some foreign country, or first take up some subject that excites us, are longings which no marriage, no travel, no learning can really satisfy."

Just like catching a glimpse of the Lord over my dance partner's shoulder is enough to make the rest of the world fade away, encounters with God produce enough joy to overshadow all the deepest longings of our hearts. God's love for us is deeper, wider, and higher than we can imagine. The satisfaction we feel in God's presence becomes greater and greater, not less and less with every encounter. It is impossible to become over-familiar with God or to get board of Him because we cannot reach the end of Him; we cannot get our fill.

David testifies to this in the Psalms repeatedly. "Weeping may tarry for the night, but joy comes with the morning." (Ps 30:5) "You make him glad with the joy of your presence." (Ps 21:6) And no matter how long he has known the Lord, David still wants more: "My soul yearns, even faints, for the courts of the LORD; my heart and my flesh cry out for the living God." (Ps 84:2)

Maybe you're in a tough season and you're having tough conversations with God about why, when, and how He's going to follow through on His promises. But we know that whatever joy is eventually granted to us in this life, it will fade unless it is the fullness of joy that comes from standing in the Presence of God. This is why Jesus urges His disciples: "remain in my love...so that your joy may be complete." (John 15:9,11)

Has anyone ever tried to talk you out of a frown? My father did that when I was a kid. After we addressed whatever was wrong, he'd say, "I see a smile," with a wink in his eye. I'd frown harder with my arms crossed. I wasn't ready to let go of how I was feeling. "You'd better not smile," he'd persist, until it was impossible not to smile! If you're sad, mad, frustrated or hurt, will you let God gently turn your frown upside down?

Here's why it matters: because "the joy of the Lord is your strength," and you may need it (Neh 8:10). The good news about great joy is that it's always available.

The Joy Set Before Us

As children, the weeks leading up to Christmas felt like delicious torture, didn't they? We couldn't stand the waiting, but the thought of the presents "hidden" in cupboards and closets had almost magical powers to cheer up even the dreariest December mornings at school. It may have been cold, the days might have been short, there may have been homework to finish and finals to study for, but we could endure just a little while longer with the thought of Christmas vacation just around the corner.

Future joy is a powerful motivator, not just for children but for adults as well. And it seems the greater the joy, the more we can endure. The early church joyfully accepted the confiscation of their property because they knew they had better and lasting possessions (Heb 10:34). Paul and Silas rejoiced in prison. It was for the joy set before Him that Jesus endured the cross (Heb 12:2).

We may not be facing prison or persecution, but we face trials of many kinds. Threats of terrorism, nuclear weapons, ecological annihilation, and social decay seem to nip at our heels with every news alert. This buzzes under the surface of human existence driving in some a fatalistic death wish and in others escapism—even religious escapism, which is the desire to go away to heaven. We are indeed people living in the valley of the shadow of death. Yet with Jesus, curious things begin to happen. The blind see, the lame walk, the dead are raised. He does not receive the leper's disease, they receive His divine health. Jesus Himself endures death and returns to life! These acts show us that:

> The kingdom of the living God is health and life and the fullness of life ...The kingdom of God is not merely an ethical ideal of righteousness and justice and peace. It is that too, but in its fullness, it is earthly and bodily and is experienced with the senses, just as the sick experience their healing and just as people who have been imprisoned outwardly and inwardly experience their liberty with all their senses. Everything that lives and has to die longs for the fullness of life in God's kingdom. (Jurgen Moltmann)

This kingdom, which Jesus proclaimed and demonstrated, is now at hand, but it is not yet fully realized, as evidenced by the dysfunction, decay, and death around us. How will this all be resolved? We are told in Revelation 21 and 22 that the New Jerusalem will come down to earth adorned like a bride. Heaven and earth once met only in the Temple. Now they meet in the hearts of believers who are filled with the Holy Spirit. But on the day when Jesus returns and heaven is married to earth, the whole world will be healed and flooded with the light of God's presence.

In John's Revelation, he hears a loud voice declare, "Now the dwelling of God is with men, and he will live with them. They will be his people and God himself will be with them and be their God. He will wipe every tear from their eyes. There will be no more death or mourning or crying or pain, for the old order of things has passed away." (Rev 21:3-5) We will sit down together at the marriage supper of the Lamb where we will celebrate the victory of God's love over the forces of death. We will receive from the Lord white stones with our true names inscribed upon them.

The battle was won the day Jesus rose from the dead. May this joy-filled present and future reality give you endurance. May it inspire you to participate in the renewing work of God's coming Kingdom until that wonderful day. May your praises open prison doors, and may the joy of your salvation give you strength.

LOVE

If I speak in the tongues of men or of angels,
but do not have love, I am only a resounding
gong or a clanging cymbal. If I have the gift of
prophecy and can fathom all mysteries and all
knowledge, and if I have a faith that can move
mountains, but do not have love, I am nothing.
If I give all I possess to the poor and give over
my body to hardship that I may boast, but do
not have love, I gain nothing. (1 Cor 13:1-3)

The candle of Love is our last stop on the Advent wreath,
and it seems the circle of branches would not hold together
without it. What good is hope for a better and peaceful
tomorrow if love is not there? What joy can there be in that
face-to-face moment when heaven meets earth if love isn't
there to greet us? I would not want to run into Jesus in the

garden if He didn't love me. It seems actually that without love, Christmas would not be good news at all.

Sometimes I worry about the world , and I imagine you probably do too. Sometimes it's in the front of my consciousness, like when in September 2016 a homemade bomb went off three blocks from my apartment. I heard the boom and thought, "That was not a truck." I didn't live in New York in September of 2001, but the aftermath and the threat and the reality of terrorism is all around us just as it is in so many other places in the world.

Other times, my worries are more like a subway train rumbling passing under the sidewalk. Nuclear threats, a steam pipe explosion on my way to work, another discouraging report about the rise in global temperatures, rockets flying from Gaza into Israel, glimpsed now by video shot by friends sharing via Instagram. These moments are arresting, troubling, they peak through my consciousness even after I have pushed them to the back of my mind because I still have to go to work and answer emails and make dinner. We feel these things deeply but sooner or later we put them away from us, too often without proper grieving, because it's too painful to hold all at once. It makes me start to wonder, does the universe care that the human race exists? Do we deserve to? Will we survive all this?

When I get discouraged about this, I re-read Jurgen Moltmann's stunning chapter, "A Culture of Life" from *Ethics of Hope*, where he names these terrors of death that threaten our existence and poses the question: is there an anthropic principle in the cosmos? In other words, does the universe care if there is intelligent life on earth?

There are only three possible answers, he says: no, a weak yes, or a strong yes. No means nature stumbled upon the human race as a happy accident or malfunction and has no particular interest or commitment to being a home for humans. A weak yes means that life self-organized and humans were born as a natural extension of its internal laws, meaning nature is inclined toward humanity's existence. A strong yes to humanity holds that in the human race, nature became conscious of itself, revealing the plans of its creator.

The message of Christianity and Christmas is God's strong yes to human life.

In the birth of Jesus and all that follows, God holds out an eternal kind of life strong enough to take away our "death wish" and awaken us from the "psychic numbing" that has been our primary means of coping with our terror of death. Jesus offers us fullness of life, resurrection life, a life-giving Spirit, and hope while we wait for this life to one day become the life of the whole earth. And this life is synonymous with the love of God, because it is in love that God presses beyond Himself to create the world, to enter the world in human life at Christmas, and it is because of love that God is committed to humanity and its perfection. In other words, according to Moltmann, we should think of "eternal life" as "loving and loved life." I'll quote Moltmann at length because I cannot say it any better:

> If God himself becomes a human being, and if
> in Christ eternal life appears among mortal men
> and women on this earth, then the human race
> is wanted by God and every individual and every
> child is desired and wanted and expected ... Right
> through the night of terror, the terror of evil, God's
> affirmation of life becomes visible. There is no
> reason to deny life, to despair of this world, or to
> give up on oneself. Even the life burdened with
> sin and given over to death will be accepted by
> God and recognized and loved as the life he has
> created. (p 59)

This life becomes possible for us because as Jesus's disciple, John, the one who calls himself the beloved disciple, explains: "God is love, and he who abides in love abides in God and God abides in him." (1 John 4:16) So you see, we cannot talk about Advent unless we talk about love.

God is love

It's such a small statement, but I think maybe I've often misunderstood it. When I read "God is love," I often equate it to mean, "God is loving. God loves me." This is true, but it's not really what John is saying. He's saying God *is* love itself.

Christians believe in the doctrine of the Trinity, the idea that God the Father, Jesus His only Son, and the Holy Spirit are three distinct persons in a perfectly united singular God. The three are united in love for one another and for the world they created. We can see them in the Genesis accounts, which again taken literally or poetically, reveals that the revelation of Jesus and the Holy Spirit in the Gospels affirms and expands upon what the people of Israel already knew in the Hebrew scriptures. At the moment of creation it wasn't just the Lord creating alone. The Spirit hovered over the surface of the deep when the earth was formless and void. It was Jesus the logos, the speaking word by which creation sprang into being. The One God of Israel is revealed as the Three-in-One God where Father, Son, and Spirit love one another in perfect unity. So God is not an enormous ego demanding worship. He is Love because He is a community of persons loving one another ferociously, faithfully, forever. And the good news of Christmas is that this Love has come for us.

But love is not always easy to accept. We're desperate for it, but feel guilty sometimes when we receive it. Since love is such a gift, I used to think that to be loved is to be in debt to someone. I'm fortunate to have loving parents and siblings. How could I ever repay them for bankrolling my existence, pouring so many resources into my life, and being my playmate and confidant for so many years? Of course I can't. But I love them back so our indebtedness is mutual.

When it comes to God, if you count yourself unworthy or can't imagine loving Him back, hearing that God loves you could trigger strange, uncomfortable feelings. I grew up singing "Jesus loves me, this I know." But along the way I picked up a low grade guilt about being loved by God and for costing Him so much. Not only have I messed up and offended Him, but He took all the expense of making things right again. I'm in over my head, I can't stand on my own two feet in this relationship. He loved me first (1 John 4:19). I owe Him so much. Slowly He's taught me to identify with the beloved in Song of Songs who confidently declares about herself, "I am the Rose of Sharon, a Lily of the Valley." He has lovingly coaxed me into receiving His love more and more in recent years.

But this summer I picked up a copy of Kierkegaard's *Works of Love* knowing that I would soon be working on this chapter. Something in the table of contents caught my attention: "Our duty to be in a debt of love to one another." This turned out to be a revelation for my understanding of God's love.

Kierkegaard sets out to understand what Paul means when he says, "Owe no one anything except to love one another." (Rom 13:8) When you give money, he explains, you're not in debt— the beneficiary owes you. If it's a loan, the borrower is in debt until they pay it back. The money you gave, no matter how much or how often, was always a finite amount. After it is paid in full, you and the debtor part ways with no other hold on each other.

Love, on the other hand, is when you feel an infinite desire to give love to another human being and to keep on giving it. The lover then takes on an infinite debt to love. It was this example that helped me understand why the lover, not the beloved, is the one with the infinite debt:

> Let us begin with a little thought experiment. If a lover had done something for the beloved, something so extraordinary, lofty, and sacrificial that we men were obliged to say, "This is the utmost one human being can do for another"—

this certainly would be beautiful and good. But suppose he added, "See, now I have paid my debt."... Would it not be, if I may say it this way, an indecency which ought never to be heard, never in the good fellowship of true love? If, however, the lover did this noble and sacrificial thing and then added, "But I have one request— let me remain in debt", would not this be speaking in love? (p 173)

Love is not a "bookkeeping-relationship". The lover chooses to remain in debt so he may keep on loving. Which means, astonishingly, that however much God may have loved me thus far, and I think we can agree that the cross was about as far as God could go, He still chooses to remain in the debt of love with me and you and all of humanity. Any effort I might make to repay Him is actually to misunderstand the nature of our relationship. In an instant I saw how my efforts to be good as repayment for His sacrifice were inappropriate, even an offense to the force and intentions of His love for me. How often were my efforts to be good a subtle way of trying to get out of debt, to lessen my dependency, and ultimately to distance myself from God? Indeed our only debt is a debt to love God and one another with the love that He first gave us. I am convinced that if we do this, our holiness will take care of itself partially now and eventually on that day when we and the whole earth are fully renewed. This is why I think Jesus told us that the greatest commandment is to love God and to love your neighbor as yourself.

There is a song I love that features a snippet of a talk by Graham Cooke who reminds us that it is God's nature to love: "He loves you because He loves you, because He loves you, because He loves you, because He loves you, because He loves you, because that is what He is like." This is what it means to really understand that God is love. As lovers, we are in a debt of love to one another and it is so delightful that we desire always to stay that way.

Can God's love be refused?

When we read through the Old Testament, we see that like every lover, God made Himself vulnerable to the misadventures of love stories gone wrong. He has felt the pain of betrayal. We see how God reacts to this through the prophet Hosea where God's wounded heart is on full display.

With tender language in chapter 11, He recounts how He has loved His people. He delivered them from Egypt, taught them to walk, took them by the arms, led them with cords of lovingkindness. They didn't know it was He who healed their wounds. He lifted their burdens and bent down to feed them. But the more He called, the further they went. They were determined to turn from Him. He's heartbroken and angry. Can you feel His agony when He says, "How can I give you up? How can I hand you over?" (Hos 11:8) His compassion prevails and He is determined: "I will not carry out my fierce anger...I will not come in wrath." (Hos 11:9)

Instead He comes to us as a child: humble, helpless, and unnoticed except by a few shepherds and wise men. This child, Jesus, who was there when the world began would endure death and, more painfully, He would endure being forsaken by His Father, who sacrificed the perfect unity of the

Trinity to defeat our worst enemy, Death, and bring us into the loving life of God forever. When you place your faith in Jesus, you literally fall into Love, which is just as thrilling and terrifying and wonderful as it sounds.

If you feel the undertow of hesitation, hear these words from Henri Nouwen in *Life of the Beloved*:

> You have lived fewer years than I. You may still want to look around a little more and a little longer so as to become convinced that the spiritual life is worth all your energy. But I do feel a certain impatience for you because I don't want you to waste too much of your time! ...Therefore I want to assure you already, now, that you do not have to get caught up in searches that lead only to entanglement. Neither do you have to become the victim of a manipulative world or get trapped in any kind of addiction. You can choose to reach out now to true inner freedom and find it ever more fully.

Made perfect in love

"There is no fear in love. But perfect love drives out fear, because fear has to do with punishment. The one who fears is not made perfect in love." (1 John 4:18)

What does perfect love look like? David Benner describes it like this: "The God Christians worship loves sinners, redeems failures, delights in second chances and fresh starts, and never tires of pursuing lost sheep, waiting for prodigal children, or rescuing those damaged by life and left on the sides of its paths."

God's love has the power to transform us. In love, He speaks to our fear of rejection, abandonment, and loneliness and says, "I love you, I will never leave your side." Suddenly we are secure. We are capable of being a friend. Lovingly, He speaks to the Ego and says, "I love you the way you are right now. You have nothing to prove." Suddenly we can be humble and happy in who we are. He speaks to our fear of scarcity and says, "I love you, I will give you everything you need." Suddenly we can be generous. So our behavior changes, but not because we are performing to get love or to repay God for His love. Obedience is the fruit of a life set free from fear and transformed by love.

How do we do we enter into this transforming love? According to psychologist and Christian author, David Benner, we surrender. We believe His loving voice, which is always a work of the Holy Spirit. As we experience His enthusiastic, reckless love for us, love for Him springs up in our hearts. But we have to trust that what God wants is our deepest happiness. If we don't believe this, we won't be able to ease the vice grip we've got on the reigns of our lives. "Surrender to God flows out of the experience of love that will never let me go. It is the response of the heart that knows since God is for me, nothing can come between me and the perfect love that surrounds me and will support me regardless of my effort, my response, or even my attention." (p 67)

The difference between striving to do this and surrendering to love, he says, is like the difference between exhausting ourselves treading water and leaning back, relaxing, and discovering that we can float. When we stop splashing about in panic, we can feel the direction of the current and more easily "go with the flow" of the Spirit.

Love is How You Know

How do we know we can believe all this? A virgin birth? Resurrection? The New Jerusalem? Doesn't this all seem rather unscientific and dubious? These are fair questions. If you are struggling to believe the resurrection of Jesus, N.T. Wright offers in his book, *Surprised by Hope*, an excellent examination of the plausibility of the resurrection. Certainly resurrection is not a normal part of this world. Jesus healed the sick and brought several who were dead back to life before His own resurrection, but we still understand these events as exceptional, outside the norm. We view Jesus's return to life as "the defining event of the new creation, the world that is being born with Jesus." (p 73) It follows that if we are going to glimpse and enter this new world, we need a new kind of knowing, a new epistemology.

We know about our world through seeing and touching, through science and history, so our first reaction to the resurrection is to examine it through the lens of our senses, using the methods of the physical and social sciences. Thomas, the famous "doubting" apostle, said he would not believe Jesus was alive unless he could see Him and touch His wounds. But when Jesus appears in their midst and offers Thomas the chance, he doesn't do it (John 20:27-28). The method he planned to use to examine the truth was suddenly totally irrelevant and Thomas is full of faith, exclaiming, "My Lord and my God!" So it is through an epistemology of faith, Wright argues, that Thomas believes the resurrection.

Peter famously denied Jesus three times on the night of His arrest, a stunning betrayal of love from the man who claimed only hours earlier that he would stand by Jesus no matter what happened. He bravely cut off the ear of the soldier arresting Jesus, but before the night was over, all his courage had melted. He saw the angry mob and the people mocking and brutalizing Jesus. He understood the threat to his life that all of this posed. As Wright puts it, "He [chose] to live within the normal world where the tyrants win in the end and where it's better to dissociate yourself from people who get on the wrong side of them." But after the resurrection, Jesus greets the disciples on the beach one morning, cooking fish over a fire. He takes a walk with Peter and asks him three times, once for each of Peter's denials: "Do you love me?" Peter says "Yes, Lord, you know that I love you" three times and is ushered into an epistemology of love that believes the resurrection from a place of encounter.

This new way of knowing, Wright argues, "involves us in new ways ... and draws out from us not just the cool appraisal of detached quasi-scientific research but also that whole-person engagement and involvement for which the best shorthand is 'love', in the Johannine sense of *agape*." Love believes the resurrection because love is able to take us outside of ourselves. In fact, Wright says, "Love is the deepest mode of knowing because it is love that, while completely engaging with reality other than itself, affirms and celebrates that other-than-self reality." (p 73) That is why the greatest experts are also the greatest lovers of their subjects. This is the epistemology of love, which is the mode of knowing in the new world where Jesus is Lord and the tyrants are not.

So love is not flimsy sentimentality or blind passion. It gives us a framework to know the truth about the coming world that we cannot discover as detached bystanders. Only through love are we able to know and embrace the otherness of God. Perhaps this is what John meant when he said, "Whoever does not love does not know God, because God is love." (1 John 4:8)

Stay in my love

"I wanted to be able to say that my life was good and beautiful. But it was not."

In the spring of 2004 I found myself in a small church in Fukuyama, Japan sitting across from the pastor, Mr. Mori. I was there to hear the story of how he became a Christian.

It was research for a writing project, and I felt terrible for being there because his wife was sick with cancer and despite my protests that I could go on to Hiroshima early, he insisted on hosting me anyway. He picked me up at the train station and we drove to the grocery store to buy food for dinner and my breakfast the next morning. Then we went to a small church where in an upstairs apartment he made dinner for me and his teenaged son. After that they left and I made my own futon on the tatami floor of the guest room. The next morning, he returned to tell me his story.

When he first posed that question of how to have a good and beautiful life, it was to high school friends one day after acting club. A young girl piped up. "I have resolved this question," she said confidently. "Come to church." He went to church with Masako but thought he could never become a Christian. Five years went by while he worked as a salaryman for a large corporation. Still he could not shake his question or his fascination with Masako's confidence. He called her parents house and tracked her down. "Have you resolved your question?" she asked when they met for lunch. He hadn't. The next time he saw her he suggested that they get married. "I wanted to keep her near me," he said. Again, she told him to come to church.

After attending church for several weeks and talking to Masako's pastor, he was discouraged. He didn't ever think he could believe in Jesus. He decided the next Sunday would be his last. He was late and sat in the back row. The pastor was preaching from John 15:9, "As the Father has loved me, so I have loved you. Now remain in my love." Mr. Mori was thinking about how small his life was compared to how big God is. He felt insignificant and discouraged, but then he heard God's invitation, *Stay in my love*, and his heart was pierced. He said it felt like a dam was broken and God's love came in.

Every time I hear John 15:9, I think of Mr. Mori and of Jesus urging us, "Remain in my love."

But how do we do this? Henri Nouwen says it requires a kind of spiritual discipline to set our hearts on the kingdom and remain in God's love. These disciplines flow in two directions: solitude and community.

In solitude, we make room in our life to be with God and to listen to Him. When Mary and Joseph traveled to Bethlehem there was no room for them in the inn, and Thomas Merton points out that this is very much the spirit of our age in his essay "The Time of No Room":

> We live in the time of no room, which is the time of the end. The time when everyone is obsessed with lack of time, lack of space, with saving time, conquering space, projecting into time and space the anguish produced within them by the technological furies of size, volume, quantity, speed, number, price, power and acceleration. (*Watch for the Light* p. 272-273)

I don't know about you, but that sounds a lot like my average Monday. Our lives are so full that there is no room for God or even for our own thoughts some days. We are filled yet unfulfilled. There seems to be nothing that fills the void in us. Yet, when the Spirit hovers over the void, it becomes as Merton says, "an abyss of creativity." Think of the Spirit hovering over the surface of the deep or overshadowing Mary. When we resist the urge towards productivity and push back the rush of thoughts, we can sit in the presence of the Lord and make room for Him. When we deny ourselves company, productive activity, and quiet our minds, it's easier to notice His presence and to be reminded of His love. This might take some experimentation to find what works best for you, but I always find it's worth it. I love how Nouwen describes the experience in his great little book *The Life of the Beloved*:

> Every time you listen with great attentiveness to the voice that calls you the Beloved, you will discover within yourself a desire to hear that voice longer and more deeply. It is like discovering a well in the desert. Once you have touched wet ground, you want to dig deeper.
> (p 37)

Love one another

With a discipline of solitude, we create space within ourselves to welcome the Spirit and receive again the gift of God's love. In community, solitude meets solitude and we receive the love of God from each other, creating spaces where God's love is on display and available to others.

It's easy to cling to other people to assuage our loneliness and defend our belonging. Communities like this defend their interests and protect themselves from outsiders. They are formed based on the attractiveness and similarities of their members. They are little tribes. They have the potential to exclude and to chip away at our feelings of belovedness. This is not the kind of community we are after.

Instead Nouwen frames community as a spiritual discipline for remaining in God's love. The discipline of Community that can help us remain in God's love is a community of individuals who have encountered God's love in solitude and who come together to listen communally to the voice of God. This may not seem much different from listening in solitude, but it is powerful. Nouwen explains in "An Invitation to the Spiritual Life":

> When we come together from different geographical, historical, psychological, and religious directions, listening to the same word spoken by different people can create in us a common openness and vulnerability that allow us to recognize that we are safe together in that word. ...Thus listening together to the word can free us from our competition and rivalry and allow us to recognize our true identity as sons and daughters of the same loving God and brothers and sisters of our Lord Jesus Christ, and thus of each other.

Nouwen even goes so far as to say that community actually makes us persons. The latin root of the word *personare* means "sounding through." In community we are revealing and calling out in each other the love of God, which is bigger than we can grasp and which sometimes we fail to see in ourselves. Only when we are doing this can we begin to remain in His love as God's people, not just as individuals. And this makes it easier for us to give God's love to others.

Love remains

At the end of days when we are face to face with God, so many of the gifts and virtues that carried us in our Christian walk on earth— prophecy, tongues, faith, hope— will have no more use (1 Cor 13:8). Our need for them will dissolve away when there is no more tension between *now* and *not yet*. On that day, there will only be *Now* and *Forever*. On that day, Love will be all that's left.

This is how John, the beloved disciple, describes the new heavens and the new earth in Revelation 21-22:

> And I heard a loud voice from the throne saying, "Behold, the dwelling place of God is with man. He will dwell with them, and they will be his people, and God himself will be with them as their God. He will wipe away every tear from their eyes, and death shall be no more, neither shall there be mourning, nor crying, nor pain anymore, for the former things have passed away." And he who was seated on the throne said, "Behold I am making all things new." ... And he said to me,"It is done! I am the Alpha and the Omega, the beginning and the end. To the thirsty I will give from the spring of the water of life without payment."

John then goes on to describe the qualities and measurements of the New Jerusalem. There will be no Temple because God Himself will live there. There will be no sun or moon because the glory of the Lord will give it light. The gates will never be shut and it will never be night. "But nothing unclean will ever enter it, nor anyone who does what is detestable or false, but only those who are written in the Lamb's book of life." (Rev 21:27)

The tree of life is there at the center of the city, just as it had been in the garden and its leaves are for the healing of the nations. This is the picture God gives us of what this unimaginable new reality will be like. You have to give yourself over to the poetry of it to appreciate it. The kingdom of God is breaking out now, and we catch glimpses of it when we pray for the sick and see them healed. We catch glimpses of it in worship when we lift our voices to join heaven's songs of praise. We catch glimpses of it when we make things fairer, when we stand in defense of the poor, when we share what we have, and we include the outsider and the widow. But it helps to be reminded of what the world will be like when Love is all that remains and when Love reigns.

The question remains, at the end of days, will you be found in Love? Has it pierced your heart?

The gospel of Luke tells us the story of two of Jesus's followers who were walking away from Jerusalem three days after Jesus's death. They were discussing their disappointment over what had happened. Now Jesus, risen from the dead but not recognized, drew near to these two and started asking them what happened. They explained how Jesus was a mighty prophet who they hoped was the Messiah but how the chief priests and rulers had Him crucified. Jesus admonishes them saying essentially, didn't you know that the Messiah would have to suffer and die? So Jesus explained to them everything the Hebrew scriptures had predicted about the Messiah and it wasn't until they reached their destination and sat down to dinner that the disciples recognized it was Jesus all along.

"Did not our hearts burn within us while he talked to us on the road, while he opened to us the Scriptures?" (Luke 24:32)

If you have come all this way and your heart is burning, let me encourage you to honor that. Ask your questions, find people you trust to talk about this with. If you're in the New York City area, the doors of Church of the City New York are open to you. There is a dinner series, called Alpha, which is exclusively for people exploring questions about faith and Christianity. You're so welcome to join us.

The Christ Candle

The white candle in the center of the wreath is the Christ candle, which is to be lit on Christmas day in celebration of the moment when God was born in flesh. In Christ we witness the fulfillment of God's promises, receive the reconciliation of God with Man with Woman with Nature, and we glimpse the new humanity that is capable of a peaceful and loving future. So Christmas is our celebration of the best news, full of great joy, for all people everywhere. I hope you'll hand this book to someone else when you're done and that you'll have a very merry Christmas.

Acknowledgements

This book exists because of the help and encouragement of dozens of people to whom I'm profoundly grateful.

To Suzy Silk Rojas and your team, thank you for editing and advising these words.

To Chris Lo and Jenice Kim, thank you for the hours of thoughtful design and illustration work.

To the leadership, creative team, and community at Church of the City New York, thank you for the prayers, encouragement, and practical support. This book is for you.

To my parents, brothers, and close friends who believed in me, thank you is too small a word.

And to Jesus, who has had my heart from the beginning, thank you for hope, peace, joy, and love.

Further Reading

I am in debt to the thinking, teaching and writing of a great number of people. The following resources are cited in these pages, and I encourage anyone who's interested to read them too.

Jurgen Moltmann, *Ethics of Hope* and
Theology of Hope
Jurgen Moltmann, "The Disarming Child" and
Thomas Merton, "The Time of No Room" from
Watch for the Light: Readings for Advent and Christmas
N.T. Wright, *Surprised by Hope*
David Benner, *Surrender to Love*
Brennan Manning, *Ruthless Trust*
Henri Nouwen, *Life of the Beloved*
Soren Kierkegaard, *Works of Love*
Hauerwas & Willimon, *Resident Aliens*
Mary Oliver, *Felicity*
Ronald Rolheiser, *The Holy Longing*

Made in the USA
Middletown, DE
19 November 2019